Sir John Franklin

FROZEN IN TIME

Unlocking the Secrets of the Franklin Expedition

OWEN BEATTIE

JOHN GEIGER

E. P. DUTTON  NEW YORK

First published in the United States in 1988 by E. P. Dutton,
a division of NAL Penguin Inc., 2 Park Avenue, New York, N.Y. 10016.

Library of Congress Catalog Card Number: 88-70265

ISBN: 0-525-24685-1

1 3 5 7 9 10 8 6 4 2

First American Edition

PICTURE CREDITS

COLOUR:

All pictures are by Dr Owen Beattie apart from: polar bear by
Lawrence Anderson; Beechey Island from Devon Island and the Beechey Island
cliffs by Walt Kowal; and Hartnell's shirt by Brian Spenceley.

BLACK AND WHITE:
Pictures on pages 6, 7, 11, 13, 14, 20, 21, 24, 33, 35, 39, 43, 101, and 141
are reproduced courtesy of the National Maritime Museum, Greenwich, England;
pictures on pages 37 and 47 courtesy of the Boreal Institute of Northern Studies,
University of Alberta, Canada; pictures on pages i and 44 from the collection of John
Geiger; pictures on pages 31 and 32 courtesy of Mary Evans Picture Library.
Maps and diagrams by Neil Hyslop.

FOR SHIRLEY F. KEEN—JG
FOR MY FAMILY—OB

CONTENTS

ACKNOWLEDGEMENTS

Acknowledgements of Owen Beattie:

So many invididuals and agencies contributed to the project in one way or another that it is not possible for me to name them all below. However, I would like to say that I have appreciated everything they have done.

The field and laboratory researches described in this book were supported by the Social Sciences and Humanities Research Council of Canada, the Boreal Institute for Northern Studies, the Polar Continental Shelf Project, and the University of Alberta. My sincerest thanks go to these agencies. Additional appreciated support for various phases of the project was received from the Park Nicollet Medical Foundation, the Science Advisory Board (NWT), Alberta Workers' Health and Compensation, the Public Affairs Office (University of Alberta) and Taymor Canada.

I would especially like to acknowledge the contributions of my Beechey Island colleagues Walt Kowal, Eric Damkjar, Arne Carlson, Roger Amy, Joelee Nungaq, James Savelle, Derek Notman, Larry Anderson, Brian Spenceley, Geraldine Ruszala, and Barb Schweger. Without their energy, insight, understanding, co-operation and dedication this book (and the research) would not have been possible. And on the King William Island portion I would like to gratefully acknowledge the assistance of Arsien Tungilik, Karen Digby-Savelle, Kovic Hiqiniq, and Mike Aleekee. My thanks are also due to Dr K. Kowalewska-Grochowska, University of Alberta Hospital; Sylvia Chomyc, Tuberculosis Control Unit, Provincial

Laboratory of Public Health (Alberta); and Netsilik Archaeology Project (James Savelle).

Finally, I would like to thank the hundreds of people who have written to me expressing interest in and support for our work, and asking for more information about Franklin, the Canadian Arctic, and anthropology. It has been impossible for me to answer all of these letters, and this book, in many respects, is my long overdue response.

Acknowledgements of John Geiger:

Eddie Keen, Rebecca J. Geiger, Dr K.W. Geiger, A.L. Gilchrist, Chris Nelson, Graham Dalziel, Dian Keen, Victor Spinetti, David C. Staples, Bob Comfort, Mary Howes, Ted Lumsden, Mel Hurtig, the *Edmonton Sun*, and also Dr Elliot T. Gelfand, Dr E.P. Schuster.

The authors would also like to thank the following: the University of Alberta libraries, the Boreal Institute for Northern Studies library, Donald Bray, Richard Daly, Tinsel Media Productions, Lucinda Vardey and Carolyn Brunton.

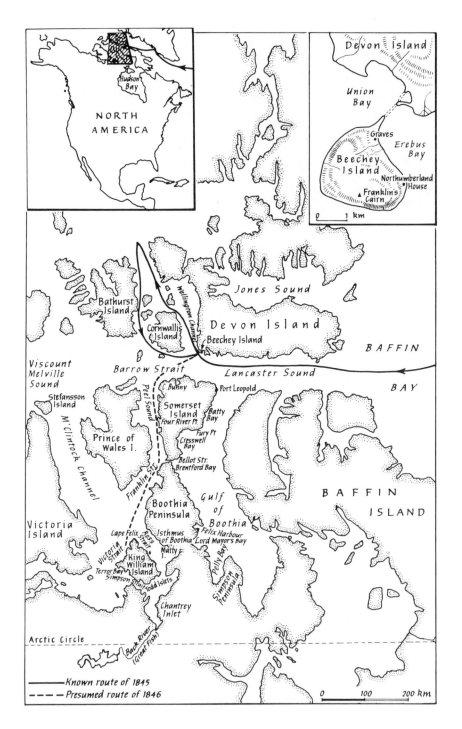

NORTH AMERICA

Hudson Bay

Devon Island

Union Bay

Graves

Erebus Bay

Beechey Island

Northumberland House

Franklin's Cairn

1 km

Jones Sound

Bathurst Island

Cornwallis Island

Wellington Channel

Devon Island

Beechey Island

BAFFIN

Viscount Melville Sound

Barrow Strait

Lancaster Sound

BAY

Stefansson Island

C. Bunny

Port Leopold

Peel Sound

Somerset Island

Batty Bay

M'Clintock Channel

Prince of Wales I.

Four River Pt.

Fury Pt

Cresswell Bay

Bellot Str.

Brentford Bay

Franklin Str.

Boothia Peninsula

Gulf of Boothia

BAFFIN

ISLAND

Victoria Island

Cape Felix

Felix Harbour

Isthmus of Boothia

Lord Mayor's Bay

Ross Str.

Matty I.

Pelly Bay

Victoria Strait

King William Island

Terror Bay

Todd Islets

Simpson Strait

Simpson Peninsula

Chantrey Inlet

Arctic Circle

Back River (Great Fish)

—————— Known route of 1845
- - - - - - Presumed route of 1846

0   100   200 km

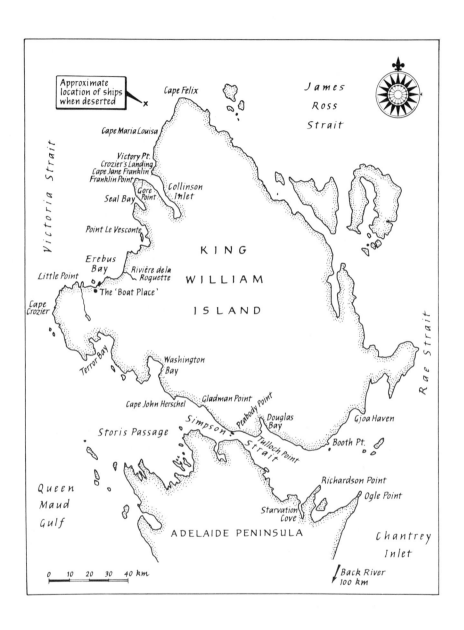

Approximate location of ships when deserted ×

Cape Felix

J a m e s *R o s s* *S t r a i t*

Cape Maria Louisa

Victory Pt.
Crozier's Landing
Cape Jane Franklin
Franklin Point
Gore Point
Collinson Inlet
Seal Bay

Point Le Vesconte

Erebus Bay
Little Point
Rivière de la Roquette

Cape Crozier
The 'Boat Place'

Victoria Strait

K I N G
W I L L I A M
I S L A N D

Rae Strait

Terror Bay

Washington Bay

Cape John Herschel
Gladman Point
Peabody Point
Simpson Strait
Douglas Bay
Gjoa Haven

Storis Passage
Tulloch Point
Booth Pt.

Queen Maud Gulf

Richardson Point
Ogle Point

Starvation Cove

ADELAIDE PENINSULA

Chantrey Inlet

0 10 20 30 40 km

Back River 100 km

FOREWORD

Climate and geography in Canada's Arctic have combined to allow researchers the inestimable privilege of discovering unique and fragile evidence of past human endeavour.

It is largely through the support of agencies such as the Social Sciences and Humanities Research Council of Canada, the Polar Continental Shelf Project, the Boreal Institute for Northern Studies and the University of Alberta that the retrieval of such information is possible.

Frozen In Time is meant to illustrate that process of retrieval, by showing how the work of a Canadian scientist and his associates is helping to explain one of the great mysteries of British and world exploration.

Most of all, though, it is an attempt to put the famous photograph of Victorian seaman John Torrington, which appeared in the international media during the autumn of 1984, into some kind of context, and to show that there were reasons for the interruption of his cold sleep.

Edmonton
August 1987

PART ONE
THE
SKELETONS

O then
Pause on the footprints of heroic men
Making a garden of the desert wide
Where Parry conquer'd death and Franklin died

CHARLES DICKENS

Chapter One

AN ARCTIC MYSTERY

Since the summer of 1848, when the long trek of an unknown British sailor from Sir John Franklin's third arctic expedition ended on the southern shores of King William Island, his bones had waited to tell their story. With every year that passed the chances of their discovery on that arctic island became more remote as the ravages of each fierce winter and the run-off from melting snow and ice each brief summer threatened to sweep them away for ever. Then, on 29 June 1981, 133 years after the sailor's death, part of a bleached human skull was discovered by University of Alberta scientists on a low spit of land that juts into the icy waters of Simpson Strait.

Franklin's finely outfitted and trained expedition ended in extraordinary tragedy in 1848. Not one of the 129 crewmen came out of the arctic wastes to tell of their accomplishments or their suffering, and both the expedition ships, HMS *Erebus* and HMS *Terror*, were lost, as were whatever written accounts of the journey that had existed. British and American searchers grasping to understand the disappearance were confounded by what little remained. Sketchy stories told by the native Inuit, and the artefacts, human remains and one tragic note found by the nineteenth-century search expeditions are all that historians have been able to rely on for their compelling yet somewhat incomplete reconstruction of events.

It was hoped the discovery by University of Alberta scientists would shed some light on the agony of the doom-struck expedition's last days, when men looked into the icy unknown for a Northwest Passage and found instead starvation and scurvy and the horrors of cannibalism. The wonder is that the bone led to much more than that. It prompted, over the next five years, three further scientific expeditions into the Canadian Arctic. With each investigation new leads were unravelled, culminating in the discovery of the preserved corpses of three of Franklin's sailors on Beechey Island. These early Victorian 'icemen' gave scientists an unprecedented look into a world very different from our own, and by opening up that past they were able for the first time to piece together accurately events leading to the destruction of the greatest enterprise in the annals of polar exploration.

Chapter Two

INTO THE FROZEN SEAS

It is hard to imagine that Sir John Franklin's mighty expedition, carrying the very best equipment that the science and technology of the day could offer, and manned by sailors from the elite Royal Navy and British merchant navy, could have ended in such tragedy.

Just three years before the last of the expedition's 129 men stumbled to their deaths at Starvation Cove on America's northern coast, when the unknown world still inspired their dreams, Franklin's crews prepared to sail the *Erebus* at 370 Imperial tons and the *Terror* at 340 Imperial tons from Greenhithe, near London. They planned to 'penetrate the icy fastnesses of the north, and to circumnavigate America'.

Franklin knew of the mysteries of the gigantic archipelago that stretches from the North American mainland towards the North Pole. This maze of land and sea presented a forbidding obstacle to those set on conquering the Northwest Passage, and the difficulties were not limited to geography. Navigators also had to contend with the crushing power of sea ice that could toss ships up on mountains of ice or just as easily pierce a vessel's hull, sending it plummeting to the depths of the Polar Sea. And then there was the bitter cold and twenty-four-hour twilight and darkness of the arctic winter.

Beginning nearly 300 years before Franklin, expeditions that sought to chart a navigable route to the riches of China and East India met only with failure. A seventeenth-century scholar compared the quest for a Northwest Passage with the legendary voyage of Jason and the Argonauts to Colchis. However, William Watts, the Cambridge scholar, noted that

Jason had found his Golden Fleece while the Northwest Passage represented 'the Searche . . . but not the finding'. None of the expeditions, from the sixteenth-century explorations of Martin Frobisher and John Davis, who chased the illusion of an open Polar Sea and trade route across the top of America, to the nineteenth-century voyages of discovery led by Captain William Edward Parry and Captain John Ross, was able to crack the lock of ice that protects the passage.

Franklin also knew of the toll of lives lost to arctic expeditions during those three centuries. In May 1619 Danish naval captain Jens Munk set out with two ships in search of a Northwest Passage. After searching along the coast of Baffin Island he entered Hudson Bay in late August and was forced to winter at the mouth of the Churchill River. There, 61 of the 64 crewmen died from the effects of extreme cold and scurvy. Munk and two of his men dumped the corpses from the

The polar regions, as perceived by Victorian England

smaller of the two vessels and managed to sail home by the autumn of 1620. Nearly one hundred years later, James Knight, a governor with the Hudson's Bay Company, sailed into the bay looking for a passage and for a treasure of precious metals he believed lay in Canada's barren Arctic. Knight's

Daguerreotype of Sir John Franklin

expedition was never seen again. Over forty years passed before its fate was finally established by Samuel Hearne of the Hudson's Bay Company. Knight and his crew had been shipwrecked on lonely Marble Island where some of the crewmen had survived for several years before they too succumbed to the cold and scurvy. Inuit later reported seeing the last two survivors of the forty-odd crew standing at the tip of the island looking in vain for signs of a relief expedition. Hearne recorded the scene:

> After continuing there a considerable time together, and nothing appearing in sight, they sat down close together, and wept bitterly. At length, one of the two died, and the other's strength was so far exhausted, that he fell down and died also, in attempting to dig a grave for his companion.

These early explorers made significant contributions to geography and science, but their discoveries carried a terrible cost. The bones of hundreds of European sailors are scattered across Arctic Canada today, tragic reminders of their lost dreams.

However, prior to the sailing of the *Erebus* and *Terror* there had been a series of nineteenth-century polar expeditions aimed at extending the frontier of the British Empire which, while experiencing failure and occasional deaths, had not suffered any large-scale loss of life. William Edward Parry contributed to the mapping of the Northwest Passage while commanding an expedition in 1819 (his first of three) through Lancaster Sound as far as Melville Island, where his two ships wintered before retreating. John Ross's second unsuccessful attempt in 1829-33 to find the passage resulted in the crew of his tiny ship HMS *Victory* being marooned on the Boothia Peninsula and Somerset Island before being rescued by a whaling vessel after four years in the Arctic. In 1844, Sir John Barrow, Second Secretary of the Admiralty, argued in support of one more attempt to complete the Northwest Passage:

> There can be no objection with regard to any apprehension of the loss of ships or men. The two ships that recently were

8

employed among the ice of the Antarctic sea after three voyages returned to England in such good order as to be ready to be made available for employment on the proposed North-West expedition; and with regard to the crews, it is remarkable that neither sickness nor death occurred in most of the voyages made into the Arctic regions, North or South.

The ships of which Barrow spoke were the *Erebus* and *Terror*. Originally designed as Royal Navy bomb vessels which could hurl explosives into land fortresses, the three-masted sailing ships had been reinforced for protection against ice for the 1839-43 Antarctic voyage under the command of Sir James Clark Ross. Ross, who as a young officer serving under his uncle John Ross on the ill-fated *Victory* became the first to reach the north magnetic pole in 1831, was sent by the Royal Navy to locate the south magnetic pole. Ross successfully chartered 800 kilometres of coastline, discovered the Antarctic ice shelf and sighted a smoking volcano, which he named Mount Erebus after his ship. A nearby crater was named Mount Terror after the smaller of the two vessels. When he returned to England in the autumn of 1843, Ross had earned himself the title of the world's leading Antarctic discoverer.

An expedition to complete the Northwest Passage was planned for the *Erebus* and *Terror* in May 1845. Ross was offered the post of expedition leader, but true to a promise he had made his wife, he declined the offer and Sir John Franklin was chosen instead. The choice of Franklin as expedition leader sparked some behind-the-scenes discussion, as he was fifty-nine years old and had not set foot in the Arctic in seventeen years. Many naval officers felt a younger, fitter man should have been given the command.

Franklin was born at Spilsby, Lincolnshire, on 16 April 1786. He entered the Royal Navy when he was fourteen, served in a number of famous battles during the Napoleonic Wars, including the Battle of Trafalgar, and was slightly injured later in a disastrous attempt to capture New Orleans in 1814. When the Duke of Wellington finally defeated Emperor Napoleon Bonaparte in the Battle of Waterloo in 1815, the

Royal Navy was forced to look for new assignments for its best young officers. Arctic exploration was one way for such officers to distinguish themselves in peacetime, and it was in May 1818 that Franklin began his polar service as second-in-command of Captain David Buchan's failed voyage into the Spitsbergen ice.

It is not known if the young lieutenant carried with him a copy of Mary Shelley's classic novel *Frankenstein*, published just two months earlier. If he had he might have shared some of the thoughts of the book's young Captain Robert Walton. Prior to his meeting with the Frankenstein monster on the polar ice floes, Walton reflected on his desire for arctic adventure:

> I shall satiate my ardent curiosity with the sight of a part of the world never before visited, and may tread a land never before imprinted by the foot of man. These are my enticements, and they are sufficient to conquer all fear of danger or death.

In 1819 Franklin again headed north, this time in command of an overland expedition ordered by the British Admiralty to travel from the Hudson Bay to the Polar Sea where he was to map North America's unexplored arctic coast. Franklin succeeded in surveying 340 kilometres of the icy shoreline east of the Coppermine River before a tragic return journey over the Canadian tundra or 'Barren Grounds' resulted in the deaths of ten men from cold and hunger, in part due to Franklin's unfamiliarity with northern conditions. Franklin himself narrowly escaped death, almost succumbing to starvation before relief arrived. When he returned to London, his account of heroic achievement marred by murder, cannibalism and his own suffering caught the public's imagination. After being promoted to the rank of captain, he returned to the area for a well-organized second overland expedition in 1825-7, resulting in his mapping another 640 kilometres of arctic shoreline, for which he was knighted.

After time in the Mediterranean and then a six-year stint as colonial governor of Van Diemen's Land, today the Australian state of Tasmania, the aging sailor was placed in command of the greatest single expedition of discovery Britain had ever mounted.

Distinguished Royal Navy officers Captain Francis Crozier and Commander James Fitzjames were also appointed to the

Captain Francis Crozier

expedition. The veteran Crozier had served in a number of earlier attempts aimed at finding both a Northwest Passage and reaching the North Pole, under the command of Edward Parry. Crozier was also second-in-command of Ross's Antarctic expedition, commanding the *Terror*. Fitzjames had served as mate aboard the first steamer successfully to navigate the Euphrates, and had served in ships operating in the Middle East and China, when he first became interested in the romantic lure of the Northwest Passage.

Although the *Erebus* and *Terror* had served Ross well, further reinforcements were made for the planned Northwest Passage expedition, including covering the bows with sheet iron. Other changes were made to assist the expedition as it made its way through forbidding arctic waters. The ships had a tubular boiler and steam-forming apparatus which conveyed hot water in a 30-centimetre-diameter pipe under the deck to warm the men's berths, and all parts of the vessels. Desalinators were built into the galley stoves.

In a revolutionary step, entire steam locomotives with specially adapted screw propellers were installed in each ship for emergency use. A 15-ton, 25-horsepower locomotive from the London and Greenwich Railway was bought for the *Erebus*, stripped of its front wheels and installed in the ship's hold. The engine of the *Terror*, at 20 horsepower, was placed in the after hold.

On 12 May 1845, *The Times* reported:

> The Lords Commissioners of the Admiralty have, in every respect, provided most liberally for the comforts of the officers and men of an expedition which may, with the facilities of the screw-propeller, and other advantages of modern science, be attended with great results.

However, filled with vast quantities of provisions and fuel, enough to last three years, the locomotives only added to the ship's congestion. Of the living quarters, only Franklin's cabin on the *Erebus* was of any significant size. Commander James Fitzjames, second-in-command of the *Erebus*, had a cabin less than 2 metres wide, while the crew of the *Erebus* were berthed in what little space remained, many slinging their hammocks alongside one another in the mess deck.

Despite the cramped quarters, the two vessels still had room for luxuries. The *Erebus* had a library of 1,700 volumes, while the *Terror* carried 1,200, including everything from narratives

Commander James Fitzjames

of earlier arctic expeditions and geographical journals to Charles Dickens' *Nicholas Nickleby* and bound copies of *Punch* magazine.

Each ship had a hand organ which could play fifty tunes including ten hymns. There were mahogany writing desks for officers, and school supplies for teaching illiterate sailors to read and write. Instruments for research in geology, botany and zoology, as well as important magnetic observations, were taken. The Franklin expedition was also one of the first voyages of discovery to carry on board a relatively new invention: a camera. No arctic expedition had ever been so lavishly outfitted.

Commander Fitzjames's cabin on HMS *Erebus*

The days before the *Erebus* and the *Terror* sailed were filled with social engagements and a general sense of excitement. Franklin and his officers were entertained at the Admiralty on 8 May. The crews were paid in advance of the sailing and it can be assumed that at least some of that money was spent at pubs dotting the docklands of the Thames. On 9 May the final official inspection of the ships took place attended by leading civil and naval figures and other specially invited guests. The *Illustrated London News* reported that 'the arrangements made for the comfort of the officers and crews are excellent. The quantity of stores taken on board is considerable.'

According to a *Times* reporter, those stores included 'numerous chests of tea, although the crews are not expected to become teetotalers, an ample supply of rum having been provided for their use in the frozen regions'.

Among the food supplies were 61,987 kilograms of flour, 16,749 litres of liquor, 909 litres of 'wine for the sick', 4,287 kilograms of chocolate, 1,069 kilograms of tea. Nearly 8,000 tins (of 1, 2, 4, 6 and 8 pounds capacity) filled with preserved meat, soups and vegetables were also provided. Other supplies loaded on the two ships were 3,215 kilograms of tobacco, 1,673 kilograms of soap, 1,225 kilograms of candles and dozens of wolf-skin blankets. Over 4,200 kilograms of lemon juice were taken and would be rationed to all during the expedition in an attempt to stave off the catastrophic effects of scurvy.

On Sunday 18 May, the eve of his departure, and with his wife and daughter present as guests, the profoundly religious Franklin read Divine Service for the first time to his crews.

On 5 May Franklin had received his official instructions: essentially to sail to Baffin Bay and Lancaster Sound through the Bering Strait, and in so doing complete a Northwest Passage, while also collecting valuable scientific and geographical information.

There were no plans for Admiralty assistance or relief should the expedition encounter difficulty and fail to complete its voyage within the three years it had been supplied for. As a cursory precaution the Hudson's Bay Company, with its fur-trading outposts at Fort Good Hope and Fort Resolution in what is now Canada's Northwest Territories, was requested to aid the expedition should word of trouble be received. The company was also instructed to alert native traders to watch for Franklin's crews.

In the last few days before he sailed, Franklin may have experienced a premonition of his fate. Suffering from the flu, he was resting at home with his wife, Jane. She had just finished embroidering a silk Union Jack for him to take. Concerned about his illness, she draped the flag over Franklin's legs for warmth. He sprang to his feet: 'There's a flag thrown over me! Don't you know that they lay the Union Jack over a corpse?'

When the expedition sailed from the Thames on the morning of 19 May 1845, carrying 134 officers and men, most felt the Franklin expedition could not fail. Franklin's only child, Eleanor, wrote to an aunt:

> Just as they were setting sail, a dove settled on one of the masts, and remained there for some time. Every one was pleased with the good omen, and if it be an omen of peace and harmony, I think there is every reason of its being true.

The expedition was already out of view when *The Times* trumpeted:

> There appears to be but one wish amongst the whole of the inhabitants of this country, from the humblest individual to the highest in the realm, that the enterprise in which the officers and crew are about to be engaged may be attended with success, and that the brave seamen employed in the undertaking, may return with honour and health to their native land.

One week later the President of the Royal Geographical Society, Sir Roderick Murchison, summed up the public mood best in a speech: 'The name of Franklin alone is, indeed, a national guarantee.'

After calling briefly at Stromness Harbour in the island of Orkney, the expedition left Britain for the last time. A transport vessel, the *Barretto Junior*, laden with stores including ten live oxen, accompanied the ships to the Whalefish Islands in Disco Bay on the west coast of Greenland, where the oxen were slaughtered for fresh meat and the supplies were transferred to the *Erebus* and *Terror*. It was from Greenland that Franklin wrote a letter in which he would say a final goodbye to Lady Franklin. It was a letter full of hope for the future:

> Let me now assure you, my dearest Jane, that I am amply provided with every requisite for my passage, and that I am entering on my voyage comforted with every hope of God's merciful guidance and protection, and that He will bless, comfort and protect you, my dearest . . . and all my other relatives. Oh, how much I wish I could write to each of them to assure them of the happiness I feel in my officers, my crew, and my ship!

Fitzjames sent home a journal in which he described the journey from Stromness to Disco as well as many of his companions, and outlined his feelings for Franklin: 'We are very happy, and very fond of Sir John Franklin, who improves very much as we come to know more of him. He is anything but nervous or fidgety: in fact I should say remarkable for energetic decision in sudden emergencies.'

The respect felt for Franklin was shared by others. Lieutenant James Walter Fairholme, a 24-year-old officer aboard the *Erebus*, wrote to his family explaining, 'he has such experience and judgement that we all look on his decisions with the greatest respect. I never felt that the Captain was so much my companion with anyone I have sailed with before.'

After saying farewell, Lieutenant Edward Griffiths, commanding the *Barretto Junior*, sailed back to Britain, taking with him four of five crewmen from the expedition who for various reasons would not make the journey. He later described the spirits of the expedition as high, and observed that the supplies, including the quality of the tinned foods, seemed quite satisfactory for the planned voyage.

A dog named Neptune and a pet monkey named Jacko accompanied the 129 sailors (four of them mere cabin boys) when, on 12 July, they pushed westward into the distant waters. Their last contact with the outside world came at the end of July, when, in Baffin Bay, they met two whaling ships, one named *Prince of Wales*, the other *Enterprise*. Franklin was waiting for conditions to allow for a crossing of Baffin Bay to Lancaster Sound. Captain Dannett of the *Prince of Wales* reported inviting Franklin and several of his officers aboard.

'Both ships' crews are all well, and in remarkable spirits, expecting to finish the operation in good time. They are made fast to a large iceberg, with a temporary observatory fixed upon it,' Dannett recorded in his log.

Captain Robert Martin of the *Enterprise* noted that Franklin said he had provisions for five years, and if it were necessary he could 'make them spin out seven years'. Martin added that Franklin told him he would 'lose no opportunity of killing birds and whatever else was useful that came in the way, to keep up their stock, and that he had plenty of powder and shot for the purpose'.

Martin was invited to dine aboard the *Erebus*, but shifting winds sent the ships apart and it was in early August 1845 that Franklin and his crew lost contact with their world. They would never come out of the new world they saw before them, a world of ice and snow.

Chapter Three

ISTHMUS OF THE GRAVES

There is no way of knowing the details of Franklin's last voyage. It is only through the courage of nineteenth-century searchers who commanded and manned several dozen major expeditions, and challenged the same ice-clogged channels and bitter cold as Franklin had, that a sketchy outline of the failed journey exists.

Unease about Franklin's disappearance first crept into the minds of officials at the British Admiralty in London by the end of 1847, but none could have guessed that their worst nightmares were already about to play themselves out on the desolation of King William Island.

With no real sense of urgency, the Admiralty sent three expeditions to relieve Sir John Franklin. Captain Henry Kellet was instructed to sail to the Bering Strait where Franklin was to break free of the arctic ice, a second expedition under the command of James Clark Ross was sent into Lancaster Sound, following the original path of Franklin, and an overland party led by Dr John Rae and Sir John Richardson was sent down the Mackenzie River in search of the 129 men. It was the failure of all three of the relief expeditions to find a trace of Franklin that finally sparked a recognition that something might have gone terribly wrong.

On 4 April 1850 the *Toronto Globe* published an advertisement announcing a £20,000 reward to be given by 'Her Majesty's Government to any party or parties, of any country, who shall render efficient assistance to the crews of the discovery ships under the command of Sir John Franklin.' A further £10,000 was offered to anyone able to relieve any of the crews or bring information leading to their relief. Finally, £10,000 was offered to anyone succeeding in ascertaining the fate of the expedition.

By the autumn of 1850 a fleet of ships was combing the arctic waterways for a sign of the missing explorers. The British Admiralty sent three expeditions consisting of a total of eight ships into the Arctic. Only one of the search expeditions, made up of HMS *Enterprise* and HMS *Investigator* under the command of Captain Richard Collinson and Commander Robert McClure, was sent through the Bering Strait. Captain Horatio Thomas Austin with second-in-command Captain Erasmus Ommanney were ordered to take their four ships into Lancaster Sound, while the third expedition led by arctic whaling master Captain William Penny was sent to the north into Jones Sound.

Lady Jane Franklin was among those active in the race to save her husband and his men, and with the help of supporters

Men of the search expedition commanded by James Clark Ross construct their winter quarters

20

sent a ship to join in the search. The United States Navy Department assisted New York merchant Henry Grinnell who outfitted two ships under Lieutenant Edwin J. De Haven, while aging explorer Sir John Ross led an expedition which had been funded by the Hudson's Bay Company and by public subscription.

The Hudson's Bay Company also sent John Rae, who was an expert in arctic survival, to assist again in the search. Rae, who travelled overland and by boat to Victoria Island, discovered two pieces of wood on the southern shore of the island, wood that could only have come from a ship. However, there was no proof that the debris was from either *Erebus* or *Terror*, and his survey ended on the south-eastern corner of the island, the ice which clogged Victoria Strait preventing him from crossing to nearby King William Island.

Finally, on 12 October 1850, the *Illustrated London News* was able to report:

> some faint gleams of hopeful light have at last been thrown upon the gloom of uncertainty which hangs over the fate of Sir John Franklin and his companions.

On 23 August 1850, Captain Erasmus Ommanney and some of the officers of the search ship HMS *Assistance* found signs of

View of the spot on Cape Riley, Devon Island, where in 1850 Captain Ommanney of HMS *Assistance* found evidence of a Franklin expedition encampment

Franklin's expedition at Cape Riley, on the south-west shore of Devon Island. After two years of disappointments the Royal Navy at last had leads in the search for the missing men. Ommanney recalled:

> I had the satisfaction of meeting with the first traces of Sir John Franklin's expedition, consisting of fragments of naval stores, ragged portions of clothing, preserved meat tins, &c . . . and the spot bore the appearance of an encampment.

But those relics told only of a brief stop, perhaps for magnetic observations early in the expedition, and nothing of Franklin's whereabouts.

Ommanney pushed on that day, combing the shoreline for clues, when a large cairn was spotted high up on the headland of a nearby islet named Beechey Island. Lieutenant Sherard Osborn, commander of the steamship HMS *Pioneer* which was also part of the Royal Navy search expedition under the overall command of Captain Horatio Thomas Austin, described the scene:

> A boatful of officers and men proceeded on shore. On landing, some relics of European visitors were found; and we can picture the anxiety with which the steep slope was scaled and the cairn torn down, every stone turned over, the ground underneath dug up a little, and yet, alas! no document or record found.

Osborn was undeterred; he still held great hope that more discoveries would follow: '[The cairn] seemed to say to the beating heart, "follow them that erected me!" '

A flotilla of search ships converged on the area, among them HMS *Lady Franklin* under Captain William Penny. The gritty Scot swore to scour the area 'like a blood-hound' until answers to the mystery were found. More traces of Franklin's crew were discovered on Devon Island, this time at nearby Cape Spencer. Penny found the remains of a hut built of stones, and artefacts including scraps of newspaper dated September 1844, a fragment of paper with the words 'until called', more food tins, torn mittens – and that was all. Then, on 27 August, a breathless sailor brought Penny startling news: 'Graves, Captain Penny! Graves! Franklin's winter quarters!'

Dr Elisha Kent Kane, ship's surgeon under American searcher Edwin De Haven, was present when the news arrived and described what happened next:

Captain De Haven, Captain Penny, Commander Phillips, and myself . . . hurried on over the ice, and, scrambling along the loose and rugged slope that extends from Beechey to the shore, came, after a weary walk, to the crest of the isthmus. Here, amid the sterile uniformity of snow and slate, were the head-boards of three graves, made after the old orthodox fashion of gravestones at home.

The tombs lay side by side in a line facing Cape Riley. Two of the grave mounds were carefully covered with limestone slabs. Their inscriptions, chiselled into the headboards, read:

Sacred
to the
memory
of
William Braine, R.M.,
H.M.S. Erebus
Died April 3d, 1846
aged 32 years
'Choose ye this day whom ye will serve'
Joshua, ch.xxiv., 15.

The second was:

Sacred to the memory of
John Hartnell, A.B. of H.M.S.
Erebus,
died January 4th, 1846
aged 25 years.
'Thus saith the Lord of Hosts, consider your ways.'
Haggai, i., 7.

The third grave, representing the earliest death, was not as carefully finished as the others. It was inscribed:

Sacred
to
the memory of
John Torrington
who departed
this
life January 1st,
A.D. 1846,
on board of
H.M. ship Terror
aged 20 years

The orderly arrangement of what Kane had called the 'isthmus of the graves' reminded Osborn of the graveyards of home:

. . . it breathes of the quiet churchyard in some of England's many nooks . . . and the ornaments that nature decks herself

The three Franklin expedition graves on Beechey Island, drawn from a sketch made by Dr E.K. Kane

with, even in the desolation of the frozen zone, were carefully culled to mark the seaman's last home.

The searchers hoped the discovery of the expedition's winter camp site and the graves of its first three victims would somehow point to Franklin's whereabouts. The dates inscribed on the headboards showed that the doomed expedition had passed the winter of 1845-6 nestled in a small bay on the east side of Beechey Island, and there was more.

Searchers sweeping the windblown island during the shortening days of late summer found other signs, including the remains of tenting sites, an armourer's forge, a large storehouse, a carpenter's house, and a few other smaller structures. Even a polar bear killed by one of the searchers revealed an earlier bullet wound. The bullet was retrieved from the beast's flesh and identified as having been fired from a rifle like those supplied to Franklin. Another large cairn was discovered, this one made of more than 700 discarded food tins filled with gravel, but nowhere was there a message telling where Franklin and his crews had sailed. The trail that began at Cape Riley on Devon Island seemed to end on Beechey Island, just 2 kilometres away.

Though death was expected on expeditions of discovery through accident or illness, three deaths during the first winter was unusual. The suggestion that the graves at Beechey Island could represent problems with the expedition's food supply was discussed by the searchers and publicly stated by Ommanney in evidence given to the British government in 1852: 'We know that 3 of their men (young men) died the first year, from which we may infer they were not enjoying perfect health. It is supposed that their preserved meats were of an inferior quality.'

Ommanney was referring to the possibility that some of the canned food was spoiled. Tinned food supplier Stephan Goldner had quality control problems with provisions supplied to later expeditions, and even before the Franklin expedition had sailed, Commander Fitzjames expressed concern that the Admiralty would buy meat from an unknown supplier simply because he had quoted a lower price.

Dr Peter Sutherland, surgeon on Penny's expedition, believing some important clues to the health and the fate of Franklin's expedition might be harboured within the graves, proposed their exhumation:

> It was suggested to have the graves opened, but as there seemed to be a feeling against this really very proper and most important step, the suggestion was not reiterated. It would have been very interesting to have examined into the cause of death; it is very probable there would be no difficulty in doing this, for the bodies would be found frozen as hard as possible, and in a high state of preservation in their icy casings.

Sutherland went on to speculate on possible causes of death for the three sailors:

> The cause of Braine's death, which happened in April, might have been scurvy supervening upon some other disease. The first two deaths had probably been caused by accidents, such as frost bite or exposure to intense cold in a state of stupor, or to diseases of the chest, where there might have been some latent mischief before leaving England, which the changeable weather in September and October rekindled, and the intense cold of November and December stimulated to a fatal termination.

Together, the rescue vessels had traced the first season of Franklin's trek from its disappearance into silence down Lancaster Sound in August 1845 until April 1846. At most they had found a partial record of the expedition's first few months beyond the reach of civilization. The searchers then prepared for a long arctic winter themselves, with no one knowing where to look next.

Chapter Four

DEATH'S ISLAND

In the spring of 1851, the search vessels sent out twenty-eight sledging parties in the hope of tracing the expedition. Man-hauled sledges visited Russell Island, Prince of Wales Island, Bathurst Island, Melville Island, Cornwallis Island, Devon Island, and Victoria Island – but search after search failed to unveil more. Thwarted, the searchers were forced to sail home to a hostile and unforgiving reception.

Despite the disappointments, expeditions continued to sail from Britain and the United States. Lady Franklin sponsored expeditions in 1851 and 1852. The first, commanded by Canadian fur trader William Kennedy in the *Prince Albert*, was sent into Regent's Inlet. The second, commanded by Edward Augustus Inglefield in the *Isabel*, was sent into Jones Sound. In addition, the British Admiralty dispatched five ships under the general command of Sir Edward Belcher in HMS *Assistance*. Henry Grinnell and George Peabody joined with United States scientific organizations to send an expedition from New York under Elisha Kent Kane in the *Advance*. Each of these expeditions contributed toward the discovery of new lands and made important observations of arctic biology, geology, and meteorology. Commander Robert McClure and his crew finally completed the Northwest Passage after abandoning their ship and walking over ice from west to east by 1854, but the mystery of what had happened to the *Erebus* and *Terror* remained unsolved.

By 1854 nine years had elapsed since Franklin had set sail on his voyage of discovery. He had provisions for three years, although it was thought the supplies could have been rationed to last some months longer. What became obvious to the Admiralty was that regardless of what more could be done to solve the mystery, nothing could be done to save Franklin and his men. On 20 January 1854 a notice in the *London Gazette* stated that unless news to the contrary arrived by the end of March, the officers and crews of the *Erebus* and the *Terror* would be considered to have died in Her Majesty's service.

Despite this, interest in the Franklin search, and in the Arctic in general, remained high in Britain. Three Inuit, or 'Esquimaux' as the Victorians called them, taken to England by a merchant, were given an audience with Queen Victoria at Windsor Castle and then 'exhibited' in London. 'The painful excitement which has so long pervaded the minds of all classes with respect to the fate of Sir John Franklin's Arctic Expedition lends additional interest to the examination of these natives of the dreary North,' the *Illustrated London News* commented on 18 February. Interest among North Americans did not always match that of the British. In one instance the *Toronto Globe* complained that only a handful of people attended a lecture on the Arctic and the possible fate of Sir John Franklin, while the same hall had been 'filled to overflowing' with those curious to view the famous midget Tom Thumb.

Finally, on Monday, 23 October 1854, under the headline 'Startling News: Sir John Franklin starved to death', the *Toronto Globe* reported 'melancholy intelligence' which had first arrived in Montreal two days earlier. After his failed earlier investigations, John Rae had made the first major discovery of the Franklin search while surveying the Boothia Peninsula for the Hudson's Bay Company. The *Globe* excitedly outlined the news:

From the Esquimaux [Rae] had obtained certain information of the fate of Sir John Franklin's party who had been starved to death after the loss of their ships which were crushed in the ice, and while making their way south to the great Fish [Back] river, near the outlet of which a party of whites died, leaving accounts of their sufferings in the mutilated corpses of some who had evidently furnished food for their unfortunate companions.

Two days later the *Globe* concluded that Rae had succeeded 'in revealing to the world the mysterious fate of the gallant Franklin and his unfortunate companions, and in proving the folly of man's attempting to storm "winter's citadel" or light up "the depths of Polar night".'

By 28 October 1854 word had reached Britain that the veil that obscured the fate of Sir John Franklin had been lifted. In a letter to the Secretary of the Admiralty, Rae outlined his discoveries:

> . . . during my journey over the ice and snow this spring, with the view of completing the survey of the west shore of Boothia, I met with Esquimaux in Pelly Bay, from one of whom I learned that a party of 'whitemen' (Kablounans) had perished from want of food some distance to the westward . . . Subsequently, further particulars were received, and a number of articles purchased, which place the fate of a portion, if not all, of the then survivors of Sir John Franklin's long-lost party beyond a doubt – a fate terrible as the imagination can conceive.

Rae went on to report second-hand descriptions of the scene, of a party of white men dragging sledges down the coast of King William Island, of the discovery a year later of bodies on the North American mainland, and evidence of cannibalism. Contrary to the *Toronto Globe* headline, there was no proof that Franklin himself had starved to death. In support of the Inuit accounts, Rae carried with him items he had been able to purchase from the natives, including monogrammed silver forks and spoons, one of them bearing Crozier's initials, and Sir John Franklin's Hanoverian Order of Merit.

Because Rae's information about the expedition's destruction came second-hand, it was obviously far from conclusive. The British government, enmeshed in the Crimean War, asked the Hudson's Bay Company to follow up the new information. Chief Factor James Anderson was able to add only slightly to Rae's report, discovering several articles from the Franklin expedition, but no human remains or records. Anderson's was to be the last official attempt to learn the fate of Franklin. Rae, although attacked by critics for not following up the Inuit reports and instead hurrying back to London, was given £8,000 in reward money, and the men in his party split another £2,000.

British public and government interest then quickly turned to the Crimean War. The very week that news of Rae's discoveries reached Britain, a confusion of orders resulted in a brigade of British cavalry charging some entrenched batteries of Russian artillery. A report in *The Times* captivated Franklin's nephew, the poet Alfred, Lord Tennyson, who immortalized the encounter where so many British horsemen died in 'The Charge of the Light Brigade'. Events had finally overtaken the disappearance of Sir John Franklin and his officers and crews, leaving many to believe that the mystery of the expedition's destruction would never be solved.

In addition, there were now others who questioned the value of research expeditions such as Franklin's, which demanded such a heavy toll. *Blackwood's Edinburgh Magazine* summed up that feeling better than any other in an article published in November 1855:

> No; there are no more sunny continents – no more islands of the blessed – hidden under the far horizon, tempting the dreamer over the undiscovered sea; nothing but those weird and tragic shores, whose cliffs of everlasting ice and mainlands of frozen snow, which have never produced anything to us but a late and sad discovery of depths of human heroism, patience, and bravery, such as imagination could scarcely dream of.

There were, however, those who had not given up on arctic expeditions, who believed that the answers to Franklin's fate lay somewhere on King William Island or on the mainland close to the mouth of the Back River. Foremost among them was Lady Franklin, who made one last passionate plea to British Prime Minister Lord Palmerston: '. . . the final and exhaustive search is all I seek on behalf of the first and only martyrs to Arctic discovery in modern times, and it is all I ever intend to ask.' She failed to convince the British government to

M'Clintock discovers a lifeboat from the Franklin expedition containing skeletons

send one final search, and launched another expedition of her own.

Lady Franklin, born Jane Griffin, became a romantic heroine in Britain because of her refusal to give up hope that searchers would one day discover the fate of her husband and his crews. Her determination, coupled with a willingness to spend a large part of her fortune to outfit four such expeditions, has haunted historians over the years as much as it inspired the searchers of her day. What makes the devotion of Lady Franklin especially moving is the recognition that she was an independent and free-thinking woman who had not married until her thirties, and saw more of the world than possibly any other woman of her day. During her long vigil, Lady Franklin not only implored the British to help, but the President of the United States and the Emperor of Russia as well. She became an expert

Lady Franklin, neé Griffin, aged twenty-four

in arctic geography, and went so far as to question incoming arctic whalers for information. One famous folk song, 'Lord Franklin', captured the passion of her search:

> In Baffin's Bay where the whale-fish blow,
> The fate of Franklin no man may know.
> The fate of Franklin no tongue can tell,
> Lord Franklin along with his sailors do dwell.
>
> And now my burden it gives me pain,
> For my long lost Franklin I'd cross the main.
> Ten thousand pounds I would freely give,
> To say on earth that my Franklin lives.

With the help of a public appeal for funds which collected £3,000 and a donation of supplies by the Admiralty, Lady Franklin purchased a steam yacht, the *Fox*, and placed command with the Arctic veteran Captain Francis Leopold M'Clintock, a Royal Navy officer who had been involved in

The *Fox* trapped in Baffin Bay, 1857/8

three earlier Franklin search expeditions. M'Clintock chose Lieutenant William Robert Hobson, son of the first Governor of New Zealand, as his second-in-command. The *Fox* sailed from Aberdeen, Scotland, on 1 July 1857.

Almost immediately problems hampered the search and the *Fox* was forced to spend its first winter trapped in ice in Baffin Bay before being freed in the spring. By August 1858 the *Fox* had reached Beechey Island where, at the site of Franklin's first winter quarters, M'Clintock erected a monument on behalf of Lady Franklin. The monument, dated 1855, read in part:

> To the memory of Franklin, Crozier, Fitzjames and all their gallant brother officers and faithful companions who have suffered and perished in the cause of science and the service of their country this tablet is erected near the spot where they passed their first Arctic winter, and whence they issued forth, to conquer difficulties or to die.

By the end of September the searchers had travelled to the eastern entrance to Bellot Strait, where they established a second winter base. From there M'Clintock and Hobson were able to leave their ship with small parties and travel overland to King William Island early in April 1859. The two split up, with M'Clintock ordering Hobson to scour the west coast of the island for clues, while he travelled down the island's east coast, then to the estuary of the Back River, before returning via the island's west coast. M'Clintock soon met up with a group of thirty to forty Inuit who inhabited a snow village on the island. After trading for Franklin relics in their possession, and questioning the Inuit, who told of finding a wrecked ship across the island and seeing Franklin crewmen who 'fell down and died as they walked along', he moved on.

M'Clintock reached the mainland and continued southward to Montreal Island, where a few relics including a piece of a preserved meat tin, two pieces of iron hoop, and other scraps of metal were found. The sledge party then turned back to King William Island, where they searched along its southern, then western coast. Ghastly secrets awaited both M'Clintock and Hobson as they trudged over the snow-covered land.

Shortly after midnight on 25 May 1859, a human skeleton in the uniform of a steward from the lost expedition was found on a gravel ridge near the mouth of the Peffer River on the island's southern shore. M'Clintock recorded the tragic scene in his journal:

> This poor man seems to have selected the bare ridge top, as affording the least tiresome walking, and to have fallen upon his face in the position in which we found him. It is probable that, hungry and exhausted, he suffered himself to fall asleep when in this position [and] his last moments were undisturbed by suffering.

Alongside the bleached skeleton lay a notebook, 'a small clothes-brush near, and a horn pocket-comb, in which a few light-brown hairs still remained'. The notebook, which belonged to Harry Peglar, a petty officer on the *Terror*, was later examined for messages. The handwriting of two individuals were found in the book, Peglar and an unknown

Lieutenant Hobson and his men opening the cairn near Victory Point, King William Island, containing the only written record of the Franklin expedition's fate

crewman. None of the messages was of importance, and some were indecipherable. Only one barely coherent passage in the handwriting of the unknown crewman, probably the skeleton M'Clintock found, seemed to refer to their desperate plight. Most of the words in the message were spelt backwards, but when corrected it read: 'Oh Death whare is thy sting, the grave at Comfort Cove for who has any doubt how . . . the dyer sad . . .'

Unknown to M'Clintock, however, the most important artefact of the Franklin searches had been located three weeks before the skeleton was found, as Hobson surveyed the north-west coast of the island. On 5 May the only written record of the Franklin expedition, two brief notes scrawled on a single piece of naval record paper, was found in a cairn near Victory Point. The first, signed by Lieutenant Graham Gore, outlined the progress of the expedition to May 1847:

28 of May 1847. HM Ships Erebus and Terror wintered in the ice in Lat. 70° 05' N. Long. 98° 23' W. Having wintered in 1846-7 at Beechey Island, in lat. 74° 43'28" N, long.90° 39' 15" W, after having ascended Wellington Channel to Lat. 77°, and returned by the west side of Cornwallis Island. Sir John Franklin commanding the expedition. All well. Party consisting of 2 officers and 6 men left the ships on Monday 24th May 1847. Gm. Gore, Lieut. Chas. F. Des Voeux, mate.

But around the margin of this paper was a second message. It was this note, dictated to Fitzjames by Captain Crozier nearly a year after the first, that in its simplicity told of the disastrous conclusion to 129 lives:

April 25th, 1848 – HM's Ships Terror and Erebus were deserted on 22nd April, 5 leagues N.N.W. of this, having been beset since 12th September 1846. The Officers and crews, consisting of 105 souls, under the command of Captain F.R.M. Crozier, landed here in Lat. 69° 37' 42" N, long. 98° 41' W. This paper was found by Lt. Irving under the cairn supposed to have been built by Sir James Ross in

H. M. S.hips *Erebus* and *Terror*
{ Wintered in the Ice in
28 of May 1847 { Lat 70° 5' N. Long 98° 23' W

Having wintered in 1846–7 at Beechey Island
in Lat 74° 43'.28" N. Long 91° 39'.15" W. After having
ascended Wellington Channel to Lat 77° and returned
by the West side of Cornwallis Island.

Sir John Franklin commanding the Expedition

Commander.

All well

WHOEVER finds this paper is requested to forward it to the Secretary of
the Admiralty, London, *with a note of the time and place at which it was
found :* or, if more convenient, to deliver it for that purpose to the British
Consul at the nearest Port.

QUINCONQUE trouvera ce papier est prié d'y marquer le tems et lieu ou
il l'aura trouvé, et de le faire parvenir au plutot au Secretaire de l'Amirauté
Britannique à Londres.

CUALQUIERA que hallare este Papel, se le suplica de enviarlo al Secretarie
del Almirantazgo, en Londrés, con una nota del tiempo y del lugar en
donde so halló,

EEN ieder die dit Papier mogt vinden, wordt hiermede verzogt, om het
zelve, ten spoedigste, te willen zenden aan den Heer Minister van de
Marine der Nederlanden in 's Gravenhage, of wel aan den Secretaris den
Britsche Admiraliteit, te London, en daar by te voegen eene Nota,
inhoudende de tyd en de plaats alwaar dit Papier is gevonden geworden.

FINDEREN af dette Papiir ombedes, naar Leilighed gives, at sende
samme til Admiralitets Secretairen i London, eller nærmeste Embedsmand
i Danmark, Norge, eller Sverrig. Tiden og Stædit hvor dette er fundet
ønskes venskabeligt paategnet.

WER diesen Zettel findet, wird hier-durch ersucht denselben an den
Secretair des Admiralitets in London einzusenden, mit gefälliger angabe
an welchen ort und zu welcher zeit er gefunden worden ist.

Party consisting of 2 Officers and 6 men
left the Ships on Monday 24th May 1847

Gm Gore Lieut
Chas F Des Vœux Mate

The notes found in the cairn at Victory Point on 5 May 1859

1831, 4 miles to the northward, where it had been deposited by the late Commander Gore in June, 1847. Sir James Ross' pillar has not, however, been found, and the paper has been transferred to this position, which is that in which Sir James Ross' pillar was erected. Sir John Franklin died on 11th June 1847; and the total loss by deaths in the Expedition had been to this date 9 officers and 15 men.

James Fitzjames, Captain HMS Erebus.

F. R. M. Crozier, Captain and Senior Officer.

and start on tomorrow, 26th, for Back's Fish River.

'So sad a tale was never told in fewer words,' M'Clintock commented after learning of the discovery weeks later. He added that the note demonstrated how the leaders of the expedition had 'met with calmness and decision the fearful alternative of a last bold struggle for life'. One mistake in the first message was quickly noted, the expedition had wintered at Beechey Island in 1845-6, and not 1846-7 as the note suggested.

When the note was completed on 25 April 1848, Fitzjames and Crozier, with their vessels trapped in ice off King William Island for nineteen months and already suffering losses never before experienced aboard ship by nineteenth-century arctic explorers, including the death of Franklin himself, had just begun a doomed march for safety.

M'Clintock described the scene where the note had been discovered:

> Around the cairn a vast quantity of clothing and stores of all sorts lay strewed about, as if at this spot every article was thrown away which could possibly be dispensed with – such as pickaxes, shovels, boats, cooking stoves, ironwork, rope, blocks, canvas, instruments, oars and medicine-chest.

Hobson found a much more vivid indication of the tragedy later when he located a lifeboat from the Franklin expedition containing skeletons and filled with relics. Men from Franklin's crew had at last been found, but the help had come ten and a half years too late. When M'Clintock later visited the 'boat place' found by Hobson, he described his tiny party as being 'transfixed with awe' at the sight of the two human skeletons which lay inside the boat. One skeleton, found in the bow of the boat, had been partly destroyed by 'large and powerful animals, probably wolves', M'Clintock guessed. But the other skeleton remained untouched, 'enveloped with cloths and furs', feet tucked into warm boots to protect against the harsh arctic cold. Nearby were two loaded double-barrelled guns, as if ready to fend off an attack that never came.

M'Clintock named the area, on the western extreme of King William Island, Cape Crozier. The boat, which had been carefully equipped for the ascent of the Back River, was 8.5 metres long, and M'Clintock estimated the combined weight of the boat and the oak sledge it was mounted on at 635 kilos.

Careful lists of the 'amazing' quantity of goods also contained in the boat were compiled. Everything from boots and silk handkerchiefs to scented soap, sponges, slippers, toothbrushes and hair-combs were found. Six books, including a Bible and *The Vicar of Wakefield*, were discovered and scoured for messages but none was found. The only provisions in the boat were tea and chocolate. M'Clintock judged the

Franklin's men lie dying beside the boat with which they had planned to ascend the Back River, King William Island.
Oil painting by W.T. Smith

39

astonishing variety of articles 'a mere accumulation of dead weight, of little use, and very likely to break down the strength of the sledge-crews'. Perhaps strangest of all was the direction in which the boat was pointing, for instead of heading towards the river that was the target of the struggling survivors, the boat was pointed back towards the deserted ships. M'Clintock guessed the party broke off from the main body of men under the command of Crozier, and were making a failed attempt to return to the ships for food.

The *Fox* returned to England in September 1859 with news of the discoveries. The success of the voyage brought both honour and fame to M'Clintock and Hobson, as well as some solace to Lady Franklin. Sherard Osborn, who had commanded a ship in an earlier search, captured the popular feeling when he wrote of Franklin:

> Oh, mourn him not! unless you can point to a more honourable end or a nobler grave. Like another Moses, he fell when his work was accomplished, with the long object of his life in view.

In Toronto, *The Globe* echoed:

> Sir John, we now know, sleeps his last sleep by the shores of those icy seas whose barriers he in vain essayed to overcome. He died, as British seamen love to die, at the post of duty. Surrounded, let us hope, by his gallant officers, who, while he lived, would minister to his every want, and when dead would bear him to his cold and lonely tomb in some rocky bay, with saddened hearts and tear-bedewed eyes.

Finally, on 15 October 1859, the *Illustrated London News* attempted to recapture the emotions felt by Franklin's sailors near Victory Point in their final desperate struggle to survive:

> Awfully impressing must it have been to Lieutenant Hobson, and subsequently Captain M'Clintock, when they thus stood upon the intrenched scene where their gallant countrymen had, eleven years previously, prepared

themselves for that last terrible struggle for life and home. Who shall tell how they struggled, how they hoped against hope, how the fainting few who reached Cape Herschel threw themselves on their knees and thanked their God that, if it so pleased Him that England and home should never be reached! He had granted to them the glory of securing to their dear country the honour they had sought for her – the discovery of the Northwest Passage.

In their last final march, the crews of the *Erebus* and *Terror* had indeed discovered the Northwest Passage. But by the time they walked along the shores of Simpson Strait, the triumph must have been a hollow one, for all around them was despair.

Franklin and his crews entered the Arctic with their primary goal the completion of the passage. Geographically there is no single passage, and on a map it is possible to plot a myriad of routes around and through the clusters of islands making up the arctic archipelago. In reality, until the advent of ice-breakers, ice conditions narrowed the possibilities to only a few choices.

By 1845, when Franklin sailed, much of the mainland coast of North America had been charted by overland explorers questing for a navigable passage, and when the ship-based explorations up to that point are added to the map of the Arctic it becomes apparent that as little as 90 kilometres of the passage, in the King William Island region, remained uncharted.

In their first season in the Arctic, Franklin's ships sailed up Wellington Channel to 77° north latitude where they were turned back either by ice or the lateness of the season. When the sailing season of 1846 began with the break-up of ice in Barrow Strait and in Erebus Bay (their winter harbour off Beechey Island), the two ships sailed roughly south and west, ending beset in the ice off the north-west coast of King William Island in September 1846. What route the ships took to reach this point is still a matter of conjecture, although it is likely the *Erebus* and *Terror* travelled through Peel Sound and what is now Franklin Strait between Somerset and Prince of Wales Islands.

Franklin believed this route would eventually lead him to parts of the mainland coastline he had explored two decades earlier. His maps told him that, in the King William Island area, he had to complete only the 90-kilometre stretch along the west side of what was then called King William's Land to be credited with completing the charting of a Northwest Passage.

The northern extent of this unknown 90 kilometres was a low point of land on the north-west coast of King William Island visited by arctic explorer James Clark Ross from the east in the late spring of 1830. Ross had named the location Victory Point. The southern extent was to be found at Cape John Herschel on the south coast of King William Island. In 1839 Peter Warren Dease and Thomas Simpson explored along the mainland coast. Moving eastward along the coast to Boothia Peninsula, they eventually turned back to the south coast of King William Island, exploring the island until they reached Cape John Herschel, where they built a large cairn. From this point they crossed back to the mainland and retraced their route to the west, a route which itself had been extended over time to Bering Strait, the western entrance to the passage.

Curiously, perhaps tragically, both Ross in 1830 and Dease and Simpson in 1839 suggested that the area they had explored, called King William's 'Land', was an extension of the mainland – a bulge of land connected directly to the south-western part of Boothia Peninsula. It is very likely that Franklin, armed with the maps, descriptions, and opinions of these earlier explorers as well as his own theories on the geography of the region, believed he had no choice in sailing direction when he eventually encountered Cape Felix, the northern tip of King William Island. Thinking that a route to the east of this point would lead to a dead end, he turned the ships to the south-west, directly into the continuously replenished pack ice that grinds down the length of M'Clintock Channel from the north-west. The power and persistence of this ploughing train of ice cannot be overestimated, and the north-west coast of King William Island bears the scars as proof. This ice mass does not always clear during the short summers and a lethal trap awaited the two ships, a trap made all the more cruel with the realization that the route along the eastern coast of the island regularly clears during the summer. It was only during their final doomed march that the surviving men from the *Erebus* and *Terror* completed the gap, and the Northwest Passage. In the words of searcher Sir John Richardson, 'they forged the last link of the Northwest Passage with their lives'.

M'Clintock's discoveries on King William Island had at last provided an outline of the expedition's last days. With this new information the final clamour for answers to the Franklin mystery died down, even though it was apparent that many questions remained. As the *Illustrated London News* was to explain on 1 January 1881: '[M'Clintock's] search was necessarily a hasty and partial one, as the snow lay thick on the ground, and the parties had to return to their vessel before the disruption of the ice in summer.'

The impetus for continuing to probe the Franklin disaster came not so much from the British but from two colourful United States citizens, who were without any arctic experience when they each began their separate searches.

The burial of Franklin depicted on the monument erected to him at Waterloo Place, London

Charles Francis Hall, a Cincinnati, Ohio, businessman who had become interested in the Arctic following the disappearance of Franklin's expedition, decided in 1859 to conduct a search of his own. Hall argued before potential backers that Franklin survivors might still be alive among the Inuit; besides, the shores of King William Island needed to be searched during the summer for more clues to the expedition's last days. After a failed first attempt to reach King William Island, Hall returned again in July 1864, finally reaching its southern coast in May 1869. Hall recorded Inuit accounts of cannibalism among Franklin's starving crews. He also recorded his anger at learning from the Inuit that, while several native families had provided an officer thought to be Crozier and a group of his men with some seal meat, the Inuit then left, ignoring pleas for further aid.

Charles Francis Hall

Thoughtlessly forgetting to add that the Inuit themselves only managed to survive at subsistence level, Hall wrote:

> These 4 families could have saved Crozier's life & that of his company had they been so disposed . . . But no, though noble Crozier pleaded with them, they would not stop even a day to try & catch seals – but early in the morning abandoned what they knew to be a large starving company of white men.

Hall also recorded Inuit reports of the location of bodies, and human remains were indeed discovered on the island's southern shores near the mouth of the Peffer River. A skeleton, later identified by a gold filling as Lieutenant Henry Le Vesconte of the *Erebus*, was collected by Hall and taken to the United States before being returned to England. Hall conducted a solemn ceremony to honour the dead man, including flying the American flag at half mast and building a monument of stones.

But much more important American discoveries were to come. On 19 June 1878, Lieutenant Frederick Schwatka, a United States cavalry officer who had served in the Indian wars of the American West at the same time as the famed defeat of Lieutenant Colonel George Custer at Little Big Horn, and who was also a qualified lawyer and medical doctor, led a tiny expedition backed by the American Geographical Society into the Arctic.

Schwatka was inspired by Hall's earlier efforts, and by American whalers who, having talked with the Inuit, reported that documents of the lost expedition might be found.

Travelling by sledge on what was to become a 5,232-kilometre return journey, Schwatka was able to reach King William Island and conduct a thorough search during 1878-9 along the route taken during the retreat of the *Erebus* and *Terror* crews. Besides confirming important aspects of M'Clintock's search, Schwatka added immeasurably to the record of relics and human remains scattered along the western and southern coasts of the island.

On 21 July 1879, Schwatka visited the boat place seen by

M'Clintock some nineteen years earlier, but instead of an intact boat and contents, he found that the site had 'evidently been thoroughly overhauled by the natives'. Besides the remnants of the boat, Schwatka found combs, sponges, toothbrushes, bottles and powder cans. He also found the widely distributed bones of four skeletons, including three skulls.

On 24 June that same summer, at what Schwatka called the 'very crest' of his long journey, near Victory Point on the island's north-west shores, an opened grave was discovered. A medal with the name of John Irving engraved on it was found at the site even though the grave had been 'despoiled by the natives some years before'. Schwatka described the scene in his journal:

> In the grave was found the object-glass of a marine telescope, and a few officer's gilt-buttons stamped with an anchor and surrounded by a crown. Under the head was a colored silk handkerchief, still in a fair state of preservation, and many pieces of coarsely stitched canvas, showing that this had been used as a receptacle for the body when interred.

Because of the original care taken in the burial, Schwatka believed the body had been buried from the ships, where a proper coffin could have been constructed. The grave site was dramatically different from the remains of so many other Franklin sailors found on King William Island, where the bones were left above ground. A human skull and other bones, thought to be Irving's, were found scattered over a wide area around the grave. 'They were carefully gathered together, with a few pieces of cloth and other articles, to be brought home for interment where they may hereafter rest undisturbed', Schwatka wrote. Of all the skeletal remains discovered by the American, only those identified as belonging to Irving were removed from the island.

Irving and Le Vesconte were the only two members of the Franklin expedition to return from the icy grasp of the Arctic to their native shores, and then it was only in death. The skeleton thought to be Lieutenant Henry Le Vesconte of the *Erebus*, collected by Hall, was entombed at a Franklin memorial in Greenwich Hospital, and Irving was buried with full naval honours at Dean Cemetery, Edinburgh.

Before leaving the Arctic, Schwatka met an old Inuk woman and her son who told a grim story of finding relics of the Franklin expedition on the shores of the North American mainland many years before, including one of the lifeboats the retreating crewmen had been dragging. Schwatka recorded the son's account:

> Outside the boat he saw a number of skulls. He forgot how many, but said there were more than four. He also saw bones from legs and arms that appeared to have been sawed off. Inside the boat was a box filled with bones; the box was about the same size as . . . one with the books in it.

The last thirty or forty of Franklin's men had apparently left the tragedy of King William Island behind them near the mouth of the Peffer River and crossed Simpson Strait, only to exhaust their last hopes in the barren reaches of an area

The grave of Lieutenant John Irving, and relics from HMS *Terror*, found by Lieutenant Schwatka

Schwatka named Starvation Cove. It has been argued that the two boxes may have contained the remains of Sir John Franklin and the expedition logs, but they have been lost for ever.

A search of the area revealed little, only the partial remains of one sailor. The Inuit explained that the land had reclaimed the rest of their bodies – that the bones had sunk into the sand and were gone for ever, mute testimony of the horror that visited the area so long ago. Schwatka's party returned to the United States in September 1880.

The *Illustrated London News* provided detailed coverage of the results of Schwatka's journey on King William Island, giving an explanation for the absence of proper graves:

> The coast had evidently been frequently visited by natives, who had disinterred those who had been buried for the sake of plunder, and left their remains to the ravages of the wild beasts . . . [Schwatka's party] buried the bones of all those unfortunates remaining above ground and erected monuments to their memory. Their research has established the fact that the records of Franklin's expedition are lost beyond recovery.

The President of the Royal Geographical Society concluded that the Franklin search expeditions had suceeded in surveying much of the arctic archipelago and 'expunged the blot of obscurity which would otherwise have hung over and disfigured the history of this enlightened age'. Despite the failure to locate the ships' records, or either of the two vessels, the Franklin searches had also pierced the Arctic long enough to answer the fundamental mysteries of the expedition's disappearance. Their route had been generally established, the reason for the abandonment of the *Erebus* and *Terror* were known, the Inuit accounts and sad discovery of relics on King William Island attested to the crews' final chilling days of life.

Canadian Arctic explorer Vilhjalmur Stefansson asked how these sea-toughened men, armed with shotguns and muskets, could have died of hunger and malnutrition so quickly in a land where the Inuit had lived for centuries, hunting with Stone Age weapons. Stefansson concluded that the chief failure of the

Franklin expedition, and other nineteenth-century British explorers of the Arctic, was in their refusal to respond to the harsh environment by adopting the survival techniques employed by the Inuit. Franklin's crews planned to survive or die civilized men, and until their desperate last days, that is what they did.

With the great search at last over, Tennyson wrote the epitaph for Franklin's memorial in Westminster Abbey:

> Not here: the white North hath thy bones, and thou
> Heroic Sailor Soul
> Art passing on thy happier voyage now
> Toward no earthly pole

Future expeditions into the polar ice would be aimed at reaching the North and South Poles. And soon other polar heroes such as Robert Peary, Roald Amundsen and Robert Falcon Scott would reach out for glory, and in doing so hold much of the world spellbound.

Britain transferred sovereignty of the arctic islands to Canada in 1880. The Northwest Passage was finally sailed by Norway's Amundsen in 1903-6 aboard a wooden sloop named *Gjoa*. It was fitting that Amundsen should have been the first, for it was the narrative of Franklin's 1819 overland journey that first led him to dream of being a polar explorer.

'Oddly enough it was the sufferings that Sir John and his men had to go through which attracted me most in his narrative. A strange urge made me wish that I too would go through the same thing', wrote Amundsen, who conquered the passage and later the South Pole, only to die in a plane crash in arctic waters.

Royal Canadian Mounted Police Sergeant Henry Asbjorn Larsen sailed the passage from west to east aboard the *St Roch* in 1940-2 and from east to west in 1944. Occasionally bones thought to belong to a Franklin expedition member were discovered during the early part of this century, but they were usually reburied. In one case, the partial skeleton of what is thought to have been a Franklin expedition member was sent to Canada's National Museum in Ottawa, where it remains in storage. By the time that Major L.T. Burwash of Canada's Department of the Interior and pilot W.E. Gilbert became the first men to fly to Crozier's Landing in 1930, there was little more than some rope and broadcloth left for them to see. Gilbert described the scene in an article published in the *Edmonton Journal* on 9 September 1930:

> Bitter winds across the still snow-covered ground made work difficult and the ravages of the tremendous storms encountered here had largely obliterated the remains of the camps in the eighty years which had elapsed.

Despite this, Owen Beattie, an assistant professor of anthropology at the University of Alberta, believed King William Island might still hold secrets of the Franklin disaster, secrets that could be exposed by the use of the latest equipment and methods employed in physical anthropology. He believed the Franklin disaster warranted at least one last pilgrimage in the interests of science. His journey, which would take two arctic summers to complete, would again follow that rock-strewn trail down which a straggling procession of British seamen had made their march to nowhere.

An aura of doom hung over desolate King William Island during the nineteenth-century visits of M'Clintock, Hall and Schwatka. For many years after the Franklin disaster evidence of the tragedy remained fresh, and with the exception of a few temporary Inuit villages on the east coast, King William Island was literally death's island. Beattie planned their survey of the island's south and west coasts to be meticulous and thorough, but 133 years had passed since the disaster and he wondered if the ghosts of the 105 men who died on the island, and at nearby Starvation Cove, still watched over their frozen ground.

Chapter Five

SCATTERED BONES

Anthropology is essentially the science of humans, comprising the biological, linguistic, social, cultural and technological origins and development of humankind. Modern science, however, has equipped a specialized branch of the field, physical anthropology, with the tools to learn the secrets of the dead by interpreting their skeletal and preserved soft tissue remains.

Owen Beattie's fascination with the field began when he read about early man at the age of ten. He still remembers the excitement that filled his mind after discovering a book on Java Man in his school library. That childhood fascination never left him. At Simon Fraser University in Burnaby, British Columbia, Beattie studied archaeology. As a graduate student he concentrated on studying the human skeleton, and advanced training required dissection courses in primate and human anatomy. His doctoral research in physical anthropology involved the analysis of hundreds of prehistoric skeletons from the north-west coast of North America, and after joining the University of Alberta in 1980 his primary interests continued to grow in the area of human identification studies, or forensic anthropology, a sub-discipline of physical anthropology.

Beattie was to apply the techniques of physical anthropology to investigations into the Franklin expedition, something no one else had attempted. Although the expedition's end is of considerable historical importance, the event was first and foremost a mass disaster. Beattie wanted to approach the Franklin tragedy as he had the carnage resulting from modern train wrecks and airplane crashes, using the same scientific techniques to attempt to establish cause of death and the identity of the dead. He planned to collect any skeletal remains found on King William Island, where most of the sailor's lives ended, and try to identify physical evidence to support or disprove the conventional view of the expedition's destruction through starvation and scurvy. He planned to look for information on health and diet, for indications of disease, for evidence of violence, and information as to each individual's age and stature. There was also a remote chance that a victim's identity could be established, through gold teeth caps or personal belongings found near a body.

Because of his special training in forensic anthropology, Beattie had assisted in numerous investigations conducted by medical examiner's offices, the Royal Canadian Mounted Police and other police forces. With his departure for King William Island, he was about to apply those tools to a far greater mystery.

Beattie set out from his cramped office on the thirteenth floor of the Henry Marshall Tory Building on the University of Alberta campus in Edmonton to investigate the Franklin expedition for the first time on 25 June 1981. He boarded a Pacific Western Airlines Boeing 727 for a flight first to Yellowknife, the capital of the Northwest Territories, then on past the Arctic Circle to the central arctic transportation centre of Resolute, a tiny community of 168 people nestled on the south coast of Cornwallis Island. Travelling with Beattie was co-investigator and arctic archaeologist James Savelle.

A truck from the Polar Continental Shelf Project picked up the two researchers at the terminal in Resolute, and they were driven to nearby barracks where they met up with field assistant Karen Digby. The Polar Shelf, operated by Canada's Department of Energy, Mines and Resources, provides a vital service by supplying scientists and researchers in Canada's far north with logistical and air support. Beattie, Savelle and Digby soon met Polar Shelf base manager Fred Alt, picked up a short-wave radio, a 30.06 rifle and a 12-gauge shotgun, and prepared for a Twin Otter aircraft to carry them into the field where they planned to retrace the steps of dying Franklin crewmen 133 years before.

Karen Digby and Jim Savelle using the 1981 survey team's canoe as a sledge to carry supplies over the ice of Douglas Bay, King William Island

Douglas Bay at 2 a.m.

Left: The Twin Otter carrying the survey team casts its shadow on the north-west coast of King William Island as it looks for a landing spot

Above: Beach ridge at Crozier's Landing where Franklin's men congregated on 25 April 1848, three days after deserting the ships, and where M'Clintock found (in 1859) some of their clothing and other relics

Right: Arne Carlson boiling water for tea at the Crozier's Landing camp site

Right: Midnight sun near Victory Point, looking out into Victoria Strait where Franklin's two ships were beset

Below: Carrying survey supplies out onto the ice of Victoria Strait and (below right) over Collinson Inlet, this time using a sledge made from twentieth-century timber and nails found at Crozier's Landing

Above: The mud flats of Erebus Bay, King William Island

Opposite above: Skeleton of a seal found on the mud flats

Right: Arne Carlson excavating the articulated skeleton of a foot at the 'boat place' on Cape Crozier, where in 1859 Lieutenant Hobson found a Franklin expedition lifeboat containing two human skeletons

Opposite below: Beechey Island viewed from Devon Island. Union Bay is to the right of the isthmus, Erebus Bay to the left

The Beechey Island grave site. The graves,
from right to left, are of: Thomas Morgan of
the *Investigator* (d. 1854); Private William Braine RM (d. 3 April 1846);
Able Seaman John Hartnell (d. 4 January 1846); Petty Officer
John Torrington (d. 1 January 1846); and a fifth, unidentified, grave

The tinned wrought iron
plaque nailed to the lid of
John Torrington's coffin.
The inscription reads:
'John Torrington died
January 1st 1846
aged 20 years'

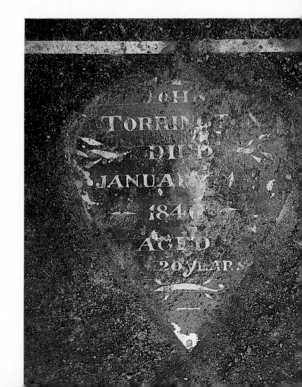

The grave of 20-year-old John Torrington after the removal of the gravel mound. Notice the row of small limestone shingles forming a fence-like feature round the grave

The coffin containing John Torrington. The arrow points to true north

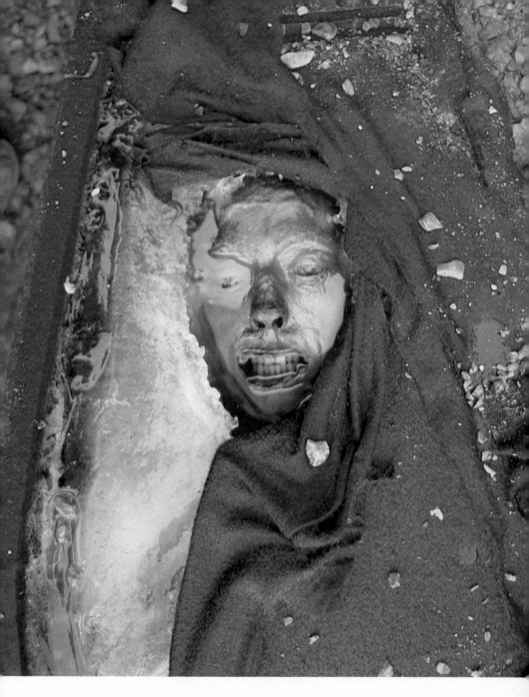

First photograph of John Torrington taken moments after the wool coffin covering was pulled back

John Torrington. The dark stain on his forehead and nose marks where his face came into contact with the blue wool coffin covering which was folded inside the coffin lid. His body was bound with strips of cotton to hold the limbs together during preparation for burial

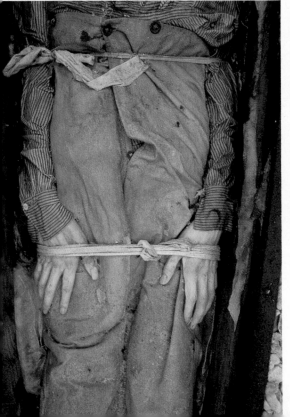

From Resolute they flew to Gjoa Haven, an Inuit community on the south-east coast of King William Island, where Inuit students Kovic Hiqiniq and Mike Aleekee joined the team as research assistants. Hiqiniq and Aleekee had helped to arrange for two hunters to carry the researchers and their equipment by snowmobile the next day south across ice-clogged Simpson Strait. There, an inlet on the North American mainland which sprawls and meanders inland for nearly 10 kilometres is named Starvation Cove and it was there that the last of Franklin's men perished.

On 27 June the five researchers made the gruelling twelve-hour journey over hillocks and cracks in the ice on *komatiks*, traditional sledges once hauled by dog teams but in their case pulled along by the snowmobiles. Sitting atop a mound of equipment and supplies, each firmly grasped hold of both sides of the komatik, as every icy obstacle along the way threatened to dislodge them. Joining them on the journey was the wife of one of the hunters carrying an infant tucked inside her warm parka. The temperature was seasonal, hovering between zero and 5°C.

Beattie and Savelle had hoped to survey Starvation Cove, looking for relics or remains of the hardiest men from the doomed expedition, but the land is extremely low, marshy, and sandy, and was almost completely covered by meltwater that summer, making their work all but impossible. While looking over the area, trying in vain to identify locations visited by Schwatka more than a century before, a lone male barren-ground caribou was spotted in the distance. The proud animal gazed at them for a time, as its ancestrors might have once done at Franklin's starving men, and then was gone.

The snowmobiles soon continued on, carrying the researchers a short distance north to a temporary Inuit fishing camp on Richardson Point. Dining that night on raw and boiled seal meat as well as raw caribou, they questioned their hosts about possible European grave sites on the south coast of King William Island. One possible grave site was described as lying on a high crest of land at Peabody Point, along their planned route.

The first actual survey work of the field season was conducted in the early morning the following day. A mist hung over them as they walked over Richardson Point, which is just 1 kilometre wide. Besides prehistoric and historic Inuit camp sites, the locations of which were mapped by Savelle, nothing was found. Disappointed that the secrets left by Franklin expedition crew members on the North American mainland would remain hidden, the five-member survey party parted company with the Inuit hunters and crossed back over Simpson Strait to the southern coast of King William Island near Booth Point, carrying all their supplies and equipment, including a canoe, themselves.

On 13 May 1869 Charles Francis Hall had visited a narrow spit of land near Booth Point with several Inuit who had reported seeing the remains of a Franklin sailor at the site. Hall recorded the visit in his journal:

> After travelling about half an hour, the party halted on a long low spit, called by the natives Kung-e-ark-le-ar-u, on which the men . . . 'knew that a white man had been buried.' This, however, was chiefly from the accounts which they had had from their people; only one of these had ever seen the grave. The spot was pointed out, but the snow covered all from view. A monument was erected, and its bearings . . . carefully noted.

Using this brief description and accompanying maps, the researchers hoped to find the human remains that Hall, because of the snow, had missed.

Walking along the gravel beaches that chilling June day in 1981, each of them carefully surveyed an assigned area for indications that the Franklin expedition had passed. Their first day of survey work on the island failed to turn up anything. It was the second morning, on 29 June, that Digby walked up to Beattie and Savelle clutching what looked like a broken china bowl in her right hand.

'I think this is something important. Is it human?' Digby asked as she handed the white skull bone to Beattie. It was the first major discovery of their field work, and represents the true starting point of Beattie's forensic investigation. Having marked the location of her find, she quickly led the rest of the excited crew to the spot. Still visible in the sandy soil was the depression where the human skull fragment had rested and, placing the discovery back in this depression, the scientists combed the narrow spit searching for other remains.

At first, only a few fragments of bone were found. But after six hours of labour, in which every centimetre of the ground was covered, the researchers had collected thirty-one human bone fragments. Most of the bone was found exposed on the surface, although some pieces were hidden by occasional pockets of soil and vegetation and others had been nearly swallowed by the sand.

The texture of the bone illustrated the severity of the northern climate. Exposed portions were bleached white, and powdery flakes of the outer bone surface cracked and fell off if handled too roughly. Sharing the exposed surfaces were little, brightly coloured colonies of mosses and lichens, anchored firmly on the sterile white of the bone as if braced for another harsh winter. By contrast, the ivory-brown underside of the bones, never exposed to the sun or elements, were found to be in extremely good condition, with all anatomical detail preserved. The researchers also discovered several artefacts at the site, including a shell button common in the early and mid-nineteenth century, and a clay pipe stem like those carried on the Franklin expedition. The skeletal remains and artefacts were found over a 10 by 15 metre area, at the centre of which lay the remnants of what had been a stone tent circle.

Carefully studying the bones while at the site, Beattie was able to identify skull features, such as the shape of the skull's frontal bone and characteristics of the eye socket, which revealed the remains to be Caucasian. Heavy brow ridges and well-developed muscle markings on the skull and limb bones identified the person as male. The skull sutures (the joints between the various bones of the skull that slowly disappear as an individual grows older) were still clearly visible, indicating that the man was between twenty and twenty-five years of age at the time of his death. Limb fragments appeared to match in anatomical detail, suggesting that a single individual was represented by the bones.

To many, skeletal remains of a Franklin sailor would have

served as an intimation of a distant Arctic disaster and that is all. But to Beattie, the discovery of the Booth Point skeleton was almost as if one of the last of Franklin's crewmen to die had come forward through time to answer some of the questions he'd been asking.

Almost immediately Beattie noted the first physical evidence to support a long-held belief among historians that expedition members suffered from the debilitating effects of scurvy during their final months. Areas of shallow pitting and scaling on the outer surface of the bones were like those seen in described cases of Vitamin C deficiency, the cause of scurvy.

The tremendous impact of scurvy was felt throughout much of the period of European expansion and maritime exploration which started in the sixteenth century. The diet of the mariners, who endured long voyages without fresh fruit and vegetables, made them susceptible to the ravages of the disease. Entire expeditions had been attacked by the deficiency disorder, often resulting in dozens of lives being lost in very short periods of time. Scottish naval surgeon James Lind first argued in 1753 that oranges and lemons be used as an antiscorbutic. Despite Lind's breakthrough, difficulties in preserving fresh foods and primitive bottling and canning techniques resulted in conditions which destroyed the vitamin, allowing the disease to remain a problem into the early part of this century.

The physical effects of scurvy can be severe, and initially include weakness, weight loss, and irritability, followed in more severe cases by swollen and bleeding gums, loosening teeth, and spontaneous haemorrhages in almost all parts of the body. The skeleton found near Booth Point left the scientists in little doubt that, during the final year of the expedition, and probably earlier, scurvy was a factor in the declining health of the crews.

During the collection of the human remains, the researchers puzzled briefly at the unusual distribution of the bones near the entrance of the tent circle. Since animal activity may have resulted in the unusual bone scatter, and much work remained to be done that day, most of their energies were directed to recording the details of their discovery. Beattie and Savelle, armed with measuring tapes and trowels, called out measurements and described the features of the rocks and bones to Digby, Hiqiniq and Aleekee, who recorded the information on a scale map and in notebooks.

Once work at the Booth Point site was complete, the survey party continued their search westward, along the south coast of the island.

The grave identified by the Inuit fishermen they had visited at Richardson Point was located at Peabody Point, but it was actually an Inuit burial from the early 1900s. Because of its more recent origin, the remains were not investigated.

At Tulloch Point, where in 1879 Frederick Schwatka had discovered what was believed to be a Franklin expedition grave, the researchers did find skeletal remains. Later Beattie and Savelle identified anatomical and cultural features confirming that it was actually the mid-nineteenth-century burial place of an adult Inuk male. Another burial site thought to have been of Franklin expedition origin, identified by Canadian explorer William Gibson in 1931, turned out instead to represent that of an adult Inuk female, also probably from the nineteenth century. Both of the latter sites were mapped and the bone samples collected for further analysis.

On 5 July, as they surveyed the coastline west of Tulloch Point, the large white dome of the Distant Early Warning (DEW) Line Station at Gladman Point came into view nearly 25 kilometres away. It was strange and a little unsettling to see this modern radar outpost in the arctic tundra. But such stations are not uncommon in the Canadian Arctic: twenty-one dot the landscape from Alaska to Baffin Island. Built in the 1950s as a line of defensive warning against air attack from the Soviet Union, the stations have been modernized in recent years and continue their function of maintaining sovereignty over Canada's airspace.

After hours of hiking, the party reached a reasonably large, slow-moving river that required the use of their canoe to cross. Once on the other side, and within 2 kilometres of the station, they began to set up camp. While Digby, Hiqiniq, and Aleekee went about this routine task, Beattie and Savelle walked up to the station. They were warmly greeted and over the next day the tired crew were treated to hot coffee, fresh fruit and showers.

It was while they were visiting the station that they learned of an amazing coincidence. A few days prior to their arrival one of the station personnel had, while hiking, discovered a moss-covered human skeleton on the surface about 1 kilometre from the station. This discovery was reported to the closest Royal Canadian Mounted Police detachment at Spence Bay. When Beattie and Savelle and their group arrived at Gladman Point, the constable stationed at Spence Bay was on his way in his own small airplane to investigate the discovery. When he arrived he met up with the surveyors. Beattie, with experience in forensic anthropology, and Savelle, an experienced Arctic archaeologist, both accompanied the constable and station personnel when they went to view the bones. As it turned out, the skeleton was that of a prehistoric Inuk male. His remains had rested above ground for hundreds of years. It was remarkable that, considering the hundreds, perhaps thousands, of people who had been to the station during its construction and period of operation, the skeleton was discovered a few days before a forensic anthropologist and archaeologist literally wandered up to the station's front door.

The Gladman Point skeleton was the last to be found that summer. Beattie returned to Edmonton in late July, disappointed that skeletons of more expedition members hadn't been located and wondering if the physical evidence of scurvy would be the only accomplishment of the survey.

Tiny pieces of the bone samples collected from both the Franklin sailor's skeleton and the Inuit skeletons were soon sent to a laboratory for trace element analysis. Use of such analysis techniques on skeletal remains is common as various elements found in bone can give information about problems in diet and possible deficiency disorders.

Then, weeks later, while Beattie and Savelle redrew maps and reviewed field notes at the University of Alberta offices, the scatter of the bones found at Booth Point returned to bother them.

Nearly all of the skull fragments had been found near a group of larger stones at what was identified as the entrance to the tent structure, while bones from the arms and legs were found more loosely scattered around the outside of the stone circle. What was initially thought to have been the remains of a sailor who had been left behind at a campsite, either near death or already dead, now began to reveal more ominous secrets.

In late September, when Beattie and Savelle were preparing the first report on the summer's research, it finally fell together: they had discovered what appeared to be physical evidence to support Inuit tales of cannibalism among the dying crewmen.

While studying the right femur, Beattie noted that three roughly parallel grooves measuring 0.5-1 millimetre in width and up to 13 millimetres in length had been actually cut into its back surface. The marks were most likely knife marks, very different from teeth marks made by gnawing animals such as foxes, wolves, and polar bears.

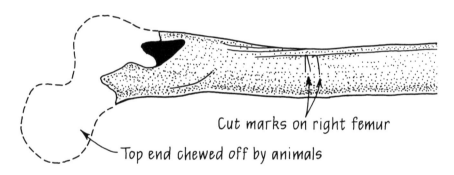

Cut marks on right femur

Top end chewed off by animals

Fracture lines also indicated that the skull had been forcibly broken; the face, including both jaws and all the teeth, was missing. Evidence that the body had been intentionally dismembered was further supported by the selective parts of the skeleton found: the head, arms, and legs. Besides the face, most of the skeleton was missing, including the twenty-four ribs, sternum (breastbone), all twenty-four vertebrae of the back, the three large bones of the hip (sacrum and two innominates), the two clavicles (collar bones) and two scapulas (shoulder blades).

Hudson's Bay Company searcher John Rae was the first to hear of the ghastly possibility. In the spring of 1854, Rae was given details of the expedition's grim final days by the natives who also had in their possession a variety of Franklin relics. Rae recorded their descriptions of a shocking sight:

> From the mutilated state of many of the corpses and the contents of the kettles, it is evident that our wretched countrymen had been driven to the last resource – cannibalism – as a means of prolonging existence.

Many Britons simply refused to believe cannibalism was possible. Charles Dickens, who followed the Franklin search closely, spoke for them when in 1854 he argued that Franklin expedition crewmen represented the 'flower of the trained English Navy . . . it is the highest degree improbable that such men would, or could, in any extremity of hunger, alleviate the pains of starvation by this horrible means'.

Dickens then attacked the source of the stories, the Inuit: [they] are covetous, treacherous and cruel . . . with a domesticity of blood and blubber'. United States Chief Justice Charles Patrick Daly, President of the American Geographical Society, went a step further, charging that Franklin was 'murdered by the Indians, who had already imbued their hands in the blood of white travellers'. But fifteen years later Charles Francis Hall too was to hear the tales of cannibalism, and this time he reported them in much greater detail.

Even today the stories are so abhorrent that they can hardly be believed. The Inuit reported finding boots filled with cooked human flesh, flesh that had been boiled. 'Some bones had been sawed with a saw; some skulls had holes in them,' Hall wrote. Other bodies found nearby had been carefully stripped of all flesh.

It is virtually impossible for those sated in their daily demands for food and drink to believe that any civilized person would intentionally and knowingly eat human brains, or consume strings of arteries, or split open bones so that the marrow could be picked out and eaten. That fact is no different today than it was in Queen Victoria's England. Yet under certain dire, life-threatening circumstances, many people would come to the realization which seems to have faced the last tattered remnants of Franklin's expedition, that cannibalism was all that stood in the way of sure death.

Modern disasters, such as the 1972 crash of a chartered plane in the Andes mountains of Uruguay, provide insights into the rationale for consuming humans for food. One of those to survive the Andes crash explained later in an interview:

> Real hunger is when you have to eat human flesh. But when you see yourself growing thinner and thinner and weaker every day and see the bones standing out and feel your eyesight dimming – you make the decision to live by whatever means possible.

Cannibalism seems to follow a pattern in instances of starvation: once the decision is made, the initial sections removed from the body are the meatier areas like the buttocks, thighs, lower legs, and arms. Recognizably human parts, such as hands and feet, are not eaten at first. As time passes and hunger continues to tear at the survivors, the options of where the flesh comes from are reduced, and bone marrow, organs, arteries, and skin are consumed. Removal of muscle tissue is usually by cutting with a knife or other sharp object, and this can leave butchering marks on the bone. Prehistoric occurrences of cannibalism associated with warface provide many examples of butchering. Removal of bone marrow requires the bone to be smashed open. The brain is either pulled through the base of the skull or eaten after the face is cut off. The need by members of Franklin's dying crew for a portable food supply was the reason for the only exceptions to this pattern.

Beattie believes a small group of the last survivors of the doomed expedition trudged eastward along the south coast of King William Island in July or perhaps August 1848. The exhausted men probably continued to hold out hope that they would reach the mouth of the Back River, from where they would attempt to travel nearly 1,500 kilometres upstream to the safety of a Hudson's Bay fort located on the eastern edge of Great Slave Lake. Slowing significantly as a result of increased exhaustion aggravated by scurvy, their food supply at an end, the sailors must have desperately looked for alternative food sources. But there were too few birds' eggs to feed the group, and hunting on the sparse northern island would have been unrewarding.

When their food finally ran out, and they were too ravaged by hunger and disease to continue, the men sat down and prepared to die. But with the first death came new hope. The survivors must have found themselves contemplating a stark fact: starvation need not be a factor any more.

Cannibalizing the trunk of the body would have given them enough strength to push on. The head, arms and legs, easily portable, were carried along as a food supply. Finally they came to a part of the island that turned sharply to the north-east – away from their goal. Camping on a small spit of land near Booth Point, the same spit of land later visited by the University of Alberta researchers, they ate their last meal. Disease and physical deterioration continued to drain them of energy as they turned southward across the ice-covered Simpson Strait, avoiding the many long, thin slivers of black sea water slicing through the ice, and the turquoise and azure pools of meltwater, making their way towards Starvation Cove. For them, the adventure and the suffering would soon be over.

Chapter Six

PHANTOMS REMAIN

In surveying the King William Island coastline the following year, Beattie, this time with field assistants Walt Kowal, a graduate student in anthropology at the University of Alberta, Arne Carlson, an archaeology and geography graduate from Simon Fraser University in British Columbia, and Inuk student Arsien Tungilik, planned to retrace the searches of M'Clintock in 1859 and Schwatka in 1878-9.

Though both nineteenth-century searchers had discovered the skeletal remains of crewmen at a number of sites, the surveyors would concentrate on Schwatka's published accounts since he had found and described more of them. He also gathered up the scattered bones and buried them in common graves at the various sites, placing stone markers on them. Beattie hoped these graves could be located, and with great anticipation plotted their supposed position using Schwatka's journals and maps. From the descriptions of bones buried at some of the sites, Beattie reckoned the number of crewmen represented at some locations could be four or more.

After a three and a half hour flight south from Resolute on 28 June 1982, the Twin Otter supplied by the Polar Continental Shelf Project swept over Seal Bay on the west coast of King William Island. Spotting a dry gravel ridge near the beach, the pilot circled back, flying close to the ground and as slow as the plane would allow. The co-pilot opened a door and with the help of Arne Carlson booted a crate filled with supplies out of the plane. All watched as the crate bounced a few times and rolled to a stop on the ridge, its pink-coloured cloth wrapping visible from kilometres away. The aircraft then headed south along the coast to Erebus Bay, where a similar procedure took place. The run-off from melting snow on King William Island made landings too risky that season, and the staff at the Polar Shelf base in Resolute came up with the idea of the air drops.

The scientific team then headed on to Gjoa Haven, where field assistant Arsien Tungilik was picked up. The Twin Otter soon flew back towards the north-west coast. After a time the pilot suddenly banked the plane to the left – he had seen a potentially good landing area in a land otherwise covered with summer run-off from melting snow. Gesturing to Beattie, he pointed out of his window to the beach ridge and nodded his head. Looking at his map, and then out of the window, Beattie nodded back that the site, about 5 kilometres north of Victory Point, would make a good starting point for the survey. After making one more low-level pass, the pilot put the plane down with metres to spare and, with one engine left running, the scientific crew jumped out of the plane's side door and began unloading their supplies. Within five minutes everything was piled up outside, and the pilot and his co-pilot pulled themselves back up into the plane. After restarting the second engine and throttling up, the plane began to move. Seconds later it was airborne and heading northward, but immediately it banked and flew past the group on the ground, the pilots waving as they set course for distant Gjoa Haven for fuel before their return to Resolute.

Although the team's food caches had been dropped along their planned route, each person's backpack was weighed down with food and supplies. Extra clothing for temperatures expected to hover around freezing point and other personal items were usually stuffed to the bottom. Next came the food, consisting mainly of packaged freeze-dried food and chocolate bars. Other important items like matches, tent and boot repair kits, first-aid kits, and ammunition were packed near the top. Sleeping bags were tied to the bottom of the packs, with a tent and sleeping pad strapped one to each side. The rifle and shotgun were attached to the top and could be reached easily while the pack was on. Other items that increased the weight of the load were the cooking utensils, stoves and fuel. A radio was carried, with which they would make twice daily contact with the base camp at Resolute. Later, when leaving a cache site, their packs would be stuffed to overflowing with supplies, and more things would be hanging from straps on the outside.

Each was burdened with a heavy pack; Beattie and Tungilik carried over 30 kilos while Carlson carried even more. But it was Kowal, a powerful man with seemingly endless energy, who served as the self-assigned workhorse for the survey party. During the first phase of the survey Beattie and Carlson had to lift Kowal's pack up to help him get it on: in it, in addition to his own belongings, he carried food, the radio, a rifle, ammunition, a sleeping bag and sleeping pad, a tent, an inflatable raft, a set of oars, two camp stoves, his camera, and, strapped to the back of the pack, a full five-gallon container of stove fuel making a total weight of over 60 kilos. Beattie was amused and amazed at the sight of Kowal as they moved along on their survey: a huge mountain of supplies appeared to be lumbering ahead on its own, powered by two legs that would disappear as he squatted down to investigate something on the ground. The mountain would then slowly rise and continue along on its course.

Loaded down as they were, each had to move slowly and conserve energy. The survey needed alert minds and inquisitive eyes; fatigue would steal those necessary qualities away. They took frequent rests supplemented by liquids (tea, coffee, hot chocolate) between each camp. With these breaks they were able to survey between 10 and 20 kilometres each day, and when searching an area out of one of their established camps, they took only the necessary supplies for one day, greatly increasing their range and speed.

Safety was an important consideration during the survey. The health services at the university had provided them with a well-stocked first-aid kit containing items like sunscreen (for face and nose), inflatable splints, bandages of all sizes, cold remedies, antibiotics, and pain killers. Apart from the remote possibility of a polar bear attack, the greatest hazards they could expect were a leg or back injury from falling or twisting an ankle. Hypothermia was also possible if any of them lost their footing while crossing one of the many streams along the route, or fell through a crack out on the ice.

Their first day on the island, and even before they had a chance to set up camp, a curious arctic fox was noticed studying them from a nearby beach ridge. Beattie thought of the brief visit by the small animal, still covered in its heavy white winter fur, as a form of welcome to the strange and exotic island they were about to encounter. Although Beattie had visited King William Island's south coast the previous year, he was now going to survey areas where humans had not been for many years.

When the fox had scurried off into the distance, the four surveyors quickly busied themselves setting up the tents of their first camp, then preparing a meal of freeze-dried food. After settling in, despite being tired from the long plane journey, they briefly explored the surrounding area. Walking inland soon brought them to a large lake, and they could see in every direction that the land was flat and virtually covered in a sheet of water.

But that first night they were to learn that King William Island can be deceiving. While the land appears absolutely flat, the reality can be quite different. It is nearly impossible to find a small patch of level ground along a coast of subtly rolling beach ridges. The result was that, during that night, their sleeping bags slipped slowly along the floor to the low end of the tent. That night on the island was not the last when Beattie would wake up several times pressed against the tent wall, forcing him to wriggle like a caterpillar back to the centre of the tent.

The following morning as they moved northward along the coast the temperature gradually warmed to 5°C: the sun emerged, and the wind shifted so that it was blowing off the island. They stopped briefly to remove their parkas, then continued the survey in shirt sleeves for the remainder of the day. The warmth of the season resulted in great quantities of meltwater flowing towards the coast from inland lakes, which made surveying conditions very difficult and almost impossible along parts of the route. Each kilometre of coastline covered usually required two or more kilometres of walking. Though their plan was to survey completely up the coast to Cape Felix, on the north-western tip of the island, they realized it would be physically impossible on foot. Therefore, when they reached a swiftly flowing stream at Cape Maria Louisa, 20 kilometres south of Cape Felix, they decided to turn south. After searching unsuccessfully for a Franklin camp site that had been discovered in the area by M'Clintock and Hobson in 1859, they camped for the night, returning to near Victory Point the next day.

Breaking camp on the morning of 30 June, the four men carried their supplies southward to the bank of another swollen stream. The depth of the water and speed of the current were too great to consider wading across, and they had to skirt round the outflow by walking out onto the ice of Victoria Strait. They wrapped their supplies in a large orange tarpaulin, tying the corners together. Then, dragging this large bundle, and burdened with their overstuffed backpacks, they began picking their way over the broken piles of ice at the waterline and out onto the smoother ice further offshore.

For the next two hours they walked, waded, and jumped over fractures and cracks in the ice and areas of open water created by the stream until they were able to angle back to the safety of the shore on the far side of the stream. After kicking off their boots and taking a well-earned rest, the survey continued south along the shoreline to the place visited by James Clark Ross in 1830 and named Victory Point.

Standing on the low rise at Victory Point and looking south, Beattie was astonished by the accuracy of the scene as depicted in an engraving made by Ross during his explorations as part of his uncle Captain John Ross's failed 1829-33 expedition. James Clark Ross described his visit:

> On Victory point we erected a cairn of stones six feet high, and we enclosed in it a canister containing a brief account of the proceedings of the expedition since its departure from England . . . though I must say that we did not entertain the most remote hope that our little history would ever meet an European's eye.

Despite the accuracy of the engraving, nothing could be found of the cairn erected by Ross. Only a small cairn erected in the middle 1970s remained.

The point is a low gravel projection into Victoria Strait, rising less than 10 metres above the high-water mark. From this spot it is possible to see Cape Jane Franklin several kilometres to the south, glazed with a permanent snow cover on its western rise, and to the west the thin, horizontal dark line of Franklin Point. Ross named these features in 1830, in the case of Franklin Point writing in his journal that 'if that be a name which has now been conferred on more places than one, these honours . . . are beyond all thought less than the merits of that officer deserve'.

In one of those instances of tragic irony, Sir John Franklin died within sight of Franklin Point seventeen years later.

Three kilometres south of Victory Point, Beattie and his small party came across another, much smaller, projection of land marking the site where the crews of the *Erebus* and *Terror* congregated on 25 April 1848, three days after deserting the ships 24 kilometres (5 leagues) to the NNW. It is this site which, along with Beechey Island, forms a focal point for the discovery of the fate of the expedition, for that note of immeasurable importance was left there, providing some of the few concrete details relating to the state and action of the crews from the wintering at Beechey Island in 1845-6 to the desertion of the ships on 22 April 1848.

Setting up camp, Beattie prepared to spend two days thoroughly researching and mapping the site, as well as surveying the surrounding area. The two tents were placed so that their doorways faced each other, and the team could sit and prepare meals and talk in their own makeshift courtyard. During their first evening there the sky and clouds to the south darkened to a deep purple and bolts of lightning flashed out from the clouds, reaching down towards the ground. Though orange sunlight still shone on their camp, the four watched with anxiety as the dark storm moved westward to the south of them. The site, known as Crozier's Landing, was so flat that their metal tent poles were prominent features – perhaps even lightning rods. They were relieved when the storm at last faded from view.

By 1982 few relics of the Franklin expedition remained at Crozier's Landing. Where piles of discarded belongings of the crewmen once lay strewn about, only scattered boot and clothing parts, wood fragments, canvas pieces, earthenware container fragments, and other artefacts could now be gleaned from among the rocks and gravel. One rusted but complete iron belt buckle was spotted by Beattie during the survey, as was a stove lid found near the spot where M'Clintock had located a stove and pile of coal from the expedition. A smashed but complete amber-coloured medicine bottle was found, as was part of the body of a clear glass bottle, complete with navy broadarrow marking, dating the artefact to Franklin.

Glass fragment showing navy broadarrow

What struck Beattie was the paucity of the remains marking this major archaeological site. How could a place with such a history of tragedy and despair shared by 105 doomed souls appear so impartial to the events that transpired during late April 1848? The artefacts that were mapped and collected in 1982 were pathetic, insignificant reminders of the failing expedition. Disturbances at the site were such that a search for the grave of Lieutenant John Irving, discovered by Schwatka, failed to turn up anything. A series of at least thirteen stone circles indicated the actual location of the tenting site established by Franklin's men. Other tent circles attested to the visits by searchers, primarily M'Clintock and Hobson in 1859, and Schwatka in 1879, and by Inuit. Evidence of more recent visits were also clearly visible: a hole excavated by Major L.T. Burwash in 1930, small piles of corroded metal fragments (possibly the remains of tin canisters), a note left by a group during an aerial visit made in August 1954, and other signs of visits made within the last decade. A modern cairn is situated at the highest point of the site (7 metres above sea level), representing the approximate location of the cairn in which the note was discovered by Hobson in 1859, and thinly scattered over the whole site are the garbage remains of our own generation.

Beattie's group made one interesting discovery as they marked with red survey tape the locations of artefacts scattered along the beach ridge. Paralleling this ridge, and towards the ice offshore, was an area of mud which, because of the time of year, had begun to thaw. Visible in the mud were coils of rope of various sizes. The anaerobic conditions of the mud, and the long period of freezing each year, had resulted in good preservation of the organic material, in stark contrast to the disintegrated rope and canvas fragments found on the gravel surface. One of the preserved coils was of a very heavy rope about 5 centimetres in diameter.

Despite this discovery, no feeling of the presence of Franklin's men at Crozier's Landing remained. It is now almost impossible to visualize that scene of bustling activity and preparation played out in growing despair. The mark of this most famous of arctic expeditions had been all but erased. Whatever ghosts once haunted the site had been carried away in the intervening years by the constant turbulent and chilling wind that blows off the ice. Beattie began to wonder if the time spent pursuing new leads into the fate of the expedition on King William Island might have been wasted.

As he stood at Crozier's Landing where the final agony of the explorers began in 1848, Beattie began to think not so much of the 105 men who died trying to walk out of the Arctic, which had until that time been his focus, but of the twenty-four others who had died earlier (including a disproportionate number of officers) while the expedition was aboard ship and food stores remained. After deserting the ships, death for the 105 survivors seemed unavoidable along the desolate shores of King William Island. It became increasingly obvious that the real Franklin mystery lay not here at its tragic end, but before.

Beattie wondered about the period from August 1845, when the expedition sailed into the arctic archipelago, until 22 April 1848 when the ice-locked vessels were deserted off King William Island. During those thirty-two lost months, nine officers, including Sir John Franklin, and fifteen seamen had died. Three had been buried at Beechey Island, while the graves of the others had never been found. Even before the ships were abandoned, the Franklin expedition had been an unprecedented disaster. John Ross and his crew, including James Clark Ross, had been forced to abandon the discovery ship *Victory* on the south-east shore of the Boothia Peninsula in the early 1830s. After four years in the arctic cold, they were finally discovered by a whaling vessel. Despite all that time in the Arctic, away from the protection of their ship and suffering the ravages of scurvy, Ross returned to England with nineteen of his twenty-two men. Beattie began to think that the most important insights into the Franklin disaster would come from the group of twenty-four who died aboard ship.

While he and Carlson mapped and collected the few artefacts found at Crozier's Landing, Kowal and Tungilik built a makeshift sledge from scraps of lumber found beside the ice edge. Round nails and the relatively fresh appearance of the wood suggested it was of very recent origin, and the two carpenters, using rocks for hammers, put it to good use. They planned to haul the camp supplies mounted on the sledge south across ice-covered Collinson Inlet to near Gore Point. Though the ice was fairly rotten and beginning to break, they reckoned that, with some care, they could save more than a week's walking by cutting across the inlet's mouth instead of going round its wet and marshy source.

Within an hour the sledge was complete and they prepared to resume their southward trek. The early evening hours were becoming cool and a silvery fog hung over the ice. The wind, usually a constant companion, had dropped to a whisper. Beattie and Carlson, who stayed behind to complete the artefact collection, watched as the other two were soon engulfed by the swirling fog, and they stood silently for ten minutes, listening to the receding sounds of the trudging footsteps and the rasp of the sledge runners.

With Kowal pulling the 150kg sledge by a rope looped around his chest, the two weaved, struggled, and fought their way across the 4-kilometre distance in four hours. Tungilik, with his superior knowledge of ice conditions, walked ahead and scouted the safest route, which Kowal followed faithfully. When they reached land they lugged the supplies up onto the beach. Though both were completely exhausted, they immediately began the arduous journey back to rendezvous with Beattie and Carlson, who were to strike out across the inlet after the artefact collection was completed.

The ice was very difficult and dangerous to cross. Parts were so soft that they would sink to their knees, and large ponds of melted water blanketed the ice surface. Wide cracks had appeared in a number of locations, and innumerable smaller cracks braided the ice. Tall, massive hummocks of snow and ice dotted the route across, and Beattie worried about surprising a bear hidden on the opposite side of one of these – a healthy paranoia that resulted in a wide berth being given to these small ice mountains.

Beattie noted that the ice they travelled over, and had seen offshore since their arrival on King William Island, was first-year ice, often little more than 30 centimetres thick. Recently, Polar Continental Shelf Project scientists using ice core samples taken from High Arctic ice caps have been able to study climate conditions over time. They concluded that the Franklin era was climatically one of the least favourable periods in 700 years, explaining the multi-year ice encountered by Franklin off the north-west coast of King William Island, ice that was sometimes over 200 centimetres thick.

Carrying packs filled with artefacts, Beattie and Carlson laboured across the ice for an hour. The fog had finally lifted and they saw Kowal and Tungilik a kilometre distant heading towards them. Within another hour they were all safely across.

On 4 July, they searched unsuccessfully for the grave of a Franklin crewman recorded by Schwatka. They also searched for the cairn at Gore Point where a second Franklin expedition note was discovered by Hobson in 1859. Virtually identical to the note found at Crozier's Landing, this contained only information on the 1847 survey party of Gore and De Vouex. There were no marginal notes on the document, though curiously the error in the dates for wintering at Beechey Island was repeated. A small pile of stones was located on the furthest projecting portion of Gore Point. As the pile was definitely of human origin and did not come from an old tenting structure (either Inuit or European), it seemed likely that the stones represented the dismantled cairn that had once held the note.

Moving southward along the coastline, the team encountered nothing to indicate the area had been visited recently, only locations marking the probable camp sites of Schwatka and his group. The next focal point in their survey was the supply cache which had been dropped from the airplane on the south shore of Seal Bay. After spending two days at this location, making good use of the stores of food and observing the dozens of seals which dotted the ice floes offshore, they surveyed the coast down to a location adjacent to Point Le Vesconte, where Schwatka discovered and buried a human skeleton. Point Le Vesconte is a long, thin projection of land which is actually a series of islets. At low tide it is easy to walk out along the point, but, as they found out, at high tide the depth of water separating the islets can nearly reach the waist.

Of all Schwatka's descriptions, the locations of two skeletons along this coast were the best documented and the most accurately identified on the survey team's maps. At Point Le Vesconte, Schwatka had recorded human bones including a skull scattered around a shallow grave containing fine-quality navy blue cloth and gilt buttons. The incomplete skeleton, of what Schwatka believed had been an officer, was then carefully gathered together and reburied in its old grave, and a stone monument was constructed to mark the spot. Yet again, the survey team failed to locate this grave, and the second one on the adjacent coastline. Beattie was disappointed. In 'curating' the skeletal remains he discovered, Schwatka had apparently marked each grave with 'monuments' consisting of just a

73

couple of stones. Along King William Island's gravel and rock-covered coastline, such graves were lost in the landscape. After scouring the area for an entire day, the frustrated party pushed on to the south.

On the morning of 9 July, Beattie turned his shortwave radio on for the daily 7 a.m. radio contact with Resolute. But instead of being greeted by the reassuring and familiar voice from the Polar Shelf base camp, only a vacant hissing sound was heard. No contact with Resolute was made that morning. The aerial was checked, the batteries changed, the radio connections and battery compartment cleaned, all in preparation for the regular evening communication.

Loss of radio contact is serious in the field; within forty-eight hours the Polar Shelf will dispatch an airplane to the last known location of the camp, bringing an extra radio and batteries. There may be a genuine emergency, but if the reason for missing radio contact is trivial, such as simply sleeping through the schedule, the Polar Shelf will put in a bill for the air time spent on re-establishing contact. An important function of the radio web twice a day is to keep track of the status of each group of scientists working in the field throughout Canada's Arctic. It is to everyone's advantage to pass along position information and plans for camp moves to the officials in Resolute.

With their radio not functioning, the team had been completely cut off from the outside world. As the group sat around discussing the consequences, they guessed it must be a radio black-out caused by solar activity – a relatively common occurrence, especially during periods of increased sun spot activity. What worried Beattie was that in their last radio contact with Resolute they had indicated they were on their way to a predetermined camp location 40 kilometres south at Erebus Bay. Loss of contact with Resolute meant there was a possibility that a plane would be sent out within the next day or two to Erebus Bay. There was some urgency, therefore, to get to that location before the plane. Three thoroughly exhausting, long days of survey and backpacking followed before radio contact was at last resumed; for those days they felt like they were the only people on earth. For all they knew, there could have been a nuclear war raging throughout the rest of the world. The absolute isolation imposed by the radio black-out was a sobering experience, one which they were not anxious to have repeated.

As they approached Rivière de la Rocquette across a dismally flat landscape, two small objects caught their attention. The first was a small grey lump that appeared in their pathway. The object soon revealed itself to be a young arctic hare, or leveret. Born fully haired, with its eyes wide open, hares are able to run just minutes after birth. This tiny, gentle animal stood out in stark contrast to the forbidding landscape. It was rigid with fright, its heart pounding. The four watched it for a time, took some photographs, then continued on. The second object turned out to be what was almost certainly an Inuit artefact constructed from material collected in the nineteenth century from a Franklin site. It resembled a primitive fishing rod made of two pieces of wood and twine. The wood was held together in part by a brass nail. It was a good example of the use made by the Inuit of abandoned European artefacts.

Surveying the coast had largely meant walking along beach ridges of limestone shingle and sloshing through shallow sheets of water draining off the island. Now, as they held their hands up to shade against the sun, the team could see the other side of Rivière de la Rocquette half a kilometre to the south-west; beyond that point the land was too flat to pick out any landmarks. The river itself posed a considerable obstacle, and there was discussion as to whether they should attempt to walk round it out on the ice of Erebus Bay. However, earlier that day they had been able to see the effect of the river's flow on the ice in the bay. The volume of water had pushed it far offshore, and the ice that could be seen through binoculars did not look very inviting. Finally, all agreed that to walk out on it would be too dangerous, so the river would have to be waded.

Beattie recalled the vivid description of Schwatka's group when they had stood on the same spot 103 years before: at that time the river was considered impassable down near its mouth, and the group had to hike inland a number of kilometres to where the river narrowed and they could cross in icy-cold, waist-deep water. Beattie wondered how he and his crew, far less rugged and experienced than Schwatka's men, would fare in gaining the far bank. Carlson and Tungilik had hip waders, which they untied from their backpacks and put on. Kowal donned pack boots that reached to mid-calf and began slowly wading out into the shallow edge of the river, searching carefully for submerged banks of gravel that would allow him to keep the water from rising above the boot tops. Tungilik struck out along the same route. Carlson and Beattie unpacked and began inflating a two-man rubber boat that they had carried (along with a set of oars) since their survey began. They planned to use it to float their supplies across the river, but Beattie also hoped to find a way to keep his feet dry. As he only had pack boots himself, it seemed reasonable to have Carlson, in his hip waders, pull him across the river in the boat. Kowal was too far away to see if he was having success in keeping dry, and the wind and distance were too great to shout to him.

Carlson and Beattie had problems inflating the boat with the rubber foot pump, and when it was half inflated the pump ceased working altogether. So, despite having a rather floppy, unmanageable water craft at his disposal, Beattie loaded his pack and climbed in. He quickly found himself floundering around before finally tumbling over on his back with his legs sticking up in the air. After a good laugh, he righted himself and, soaked, climbed out of the boat. He and Carlson started wading slowly across after the others, the empty and limp boat bobbing and swivelling downstream from a rope attached to Carlson's pack. The water turned out to be very shallow almost the whole distance across, though within 50 metres of the other side it increased to knee depth.

Resting by a rock near the river bank the four looked off to the west across a forbidding 10 kilometres of mud flats. Their next stop would be the food cache they had dropped from the airplane on the first day of the season. They needed to replenish their supplies: for the past two days they had virtually run out of food and fuel, and they were looking forward to the supplies they had packed in the distant cache. So, thinking as much about their empty stomachs as the obviously difficult walk before them, they struck out into the grey-brown featureless mud flats.

Immediately they encountered difficulty in walking. The clay-like mud had melted down 10 centimetres or more and was softy and pasty. Each footstep squeezed the mud out like toothpaste. And the friction and suction of the mud made extracting the foot a struggle. At first their feet sank in only up to their boot tops, but as they pushed a few more kilometres out onto the flats there was more water in the mud. Now their feet sank down to the permafrost. The grip of the mud, sometimes ankle deep but at other times more than knee deep, was so strong that they often pulled their feet right out of their boots.

At times they would encounter an island of vegetation where the footing was good, and at each of these spots they would take a short rest before plunging into the mud again. In one of these 'islands' the intact skeleton of a bearded seal was found. Virtually undisturbed by animals, it looked almost surreal against the backdrop of the mudflats.

Halfway across they began to see the slightly raised beach ridge which marked the location where they had dropped their cache, and two hours later when they finally started up the nearly imperceptible slope of the western extent of the flats they were within only a few kilometres of their next camp. When at last they reached firm ground, they threw their packs down and sat to rest their legs.

It had taken more than four hours to cross the flats. Although the cold wind blew persistently off the ice at Erebus Bay, the day was sunny and warm, nearly 10°C, and before long all were lying on their backs, soaking in the sun, thankful that they did not have to return by the same route. Twenty minutes passed with hardly a word said before one of them, Carlson, finally sat up. He started busying himself with his pack. Their bodies now rested, stomachs began to growl: the next goal was the cache.

Walking to the west they dropped quickly down into another flat area, but this one was only 1 kilometre across and had good footing. Several pairs of whistling swans, which had constructed their large nests there, could be seen nearby. After a pause to observe the large and majestic birds, the four men continued on their long walk. Then, in the middle of the flats,

Tungilik stopped dead and, pointing at the ground, asked Kowal, 'What's this bone?' Kowal was shocked to see a right human tibia lying on the surface. He called to Beattie and Carlson who had been following 200 metres behind. As the others hurried toward them Kowal decided to have some fun. He quickly covered the bone with a piece of driftwood he found nearby. When Beattie and Carlson finally arrived, both panting under the weight of their packs, Kowal said, 'Look at this!' Beattie looked down at the wood, and said, 'You made me hurry up for this?' Then, turning it over with his foot, a broad smile crossed his face. All thought of reaching the food cache quickly vanished as they began searching the location for other bones. Five more were found nearby, as were two weathered pieces of wood planking, one of which had remnants of green paint, a brass screw and badly rusted iron nail shafts. Because the six bones were from different parts of the skeleton, it seemed likely that they were from one person. However, since none of the bones was from the skull, it was not possible to tell whether the person was European or Inuk, but Beattie felt that the bones were close enough to the location of the lifeboat first found by M'Clintock that they probably represented a Franklin crewman. The wood planking supported this interpretation.

The bones were photographed, described and then collected, and the location marked on the team's maps. Elated with their discovery, and feeling renewed confidence that the area of the boat would yield new and important information, they continued at an increased pace. When they saw the bright pink bundles of supplies in the distance, they broke into a jog and, if the packs had allowed, they would probably have raced the last few hundred metres to their cache. Reaching the bundles almost simultaneously, they unslung their packs, rummaged quickly to locate their knives, and within seconds were all slashing away at a claimed bundle. They each searched for their favourite food: Kowal was looking for the boxes of chocolate-covered macaroon candy bars, Tungilik the cans of roast beef, Beattie the tins of herring, and Carlson the canned tuna. With hardly a word to each other they dug into their food, sitting on the sandy beach ridge among the debris of their haphazard and comically frenzied search for food. The sounds of chewing, the crackle of plastic wrappers, and the scraping of cans were interrupted by Kowal: 'Can you believe us?' he said, looking up from a near-empty package, a chocolate macaroon poised in his right hand. 'And we're not even starving. Those poor guys must have really suffered.'

On 12 July the surveyors headed out from their newly established base camps. They found nothing more in the area where they had discovered the six bones, just 1 kilometre from their camp, but 3 kilometres to the west of the camp they discovered a 30 by 40 metre area littered with wood fragments, and as they closely searched the site, larger pieces of wood were found. Schwatka's description of the coastline and the small islands a few hundred metres out into Erebus Bay left little doubt that they had reached the boat place where the large lifeboat from the Franklin expedition, filled with relics, was first discovered by M'Clintock and Hobson in 1859, and later visited by Schwatka in 1879. But the sight which had filled M'Clintock and the others with awe so many years before had vanished: the skeletons that once stood guard over their final resting place were nowhere to be seen. An exhaustive search of the site was conducted, and slowly, out of the gravel, came bits and pieces that both touched the researchers and graphically demonstrated to them the heavy toll of lives once claimed by the barrenlands of King William Island.

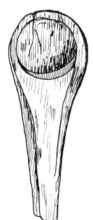

Cherrywood pipe

In the immediate vicinity they eventually located many artefacts, including a barrel stave, a wood paddle handle, boot parts, and a cherrywood pipe bowl and stem similar to those found by M'Clintock at the same site.

Most important, however, was the discovery of human skeletal remains. From the boat place, scattered along the coast for a kilometre to the north, they found bones from the shoulder (scapulas) and leg (femurs, tibias). M'Clintock had argued that, as the lifeboat was found pointing directly at the next northerly point of land, it was obviously being pulled back towards the deserted ships, possibly for more supplies. In 1982 discoveries at the boat place tended to support this interpretation: the human skeletal remains were found scattered from the location of the lifeboat towards the ships, as if those pulling the lifeboat could go no further, abandoned the lifeboat, and themselves died a short time later as they walked towards the ships. Several of the bones showed scarring due to scurvy similar to that discovered among the remains found a year earlier near Booth Point. Signs of gnawing supported the theory that animals scattered the bones of some of the crewmen who died near the boat, and Beattie suspected the possibility of past human disturbance was equally high.

The team worked long and hard, each of the four men combing the ground for any relic or human bone. Dusk soon surrounded them, but no nightfall follows dusk during the summer at such high latitudes. It was under the midnight sun that Tungilik made the survey's most important find.

While systematically searching the boat place, Tungilik caught site of a small ivory-white object projecting slightly from a mat of vegetation. Picking at the object with his finger, out popped a human talus (ankle bone). With his trowel, Carlson scraped the delicate, dark green vegetation aside, revealing a series of bones immediately recognizable as a virtually complete human foot. Continuing his excavation, which lasted into the early-morning hours of 13 July, Carlson found most of the thirteen bones from the left foot were articulated, or still in place, meaning that the foot had come to rest at this spot and had not been disturbed since 1848. The skeletal remains varied from a calcaneus, or heel bone, measuring 8 centimetres long, to a tiny sesamoid bone no bigger than 3 millimetres across. Also found was part of the right foot from the same person, which supported the interpretation that a whole body may have rested on the surface at this spot.

In all, the remains of between six and fourteen individuals were located in the area of the boat place. In determining the minimum number of individuals from the collection of bones, Beattie first looked to see how many of the bones were duplicated. Then he examined their anatomy, such as size and muscle attachment markings, comparing bones from the left and right sides of the body to see if they were from one or more individuals.

Beattie was sure that the bones had been missed by Schwatka. From his journal, it is obvious that Schwatka was reasonably thorough in his collection of bones. He had discovered the skull and long bones of at least four individuals, and buried these at the site. As in the previous searches along the coast that summer, Beattie and his crew were not able to find this grave. Of the bones discovered by the scientists in 1982, no skull bones were found.

Strangely, the most touching discovery made at the boat place was not a bone, but an artefact found by Kowal. Surveying a beach ridge further inland on 13 July he saw, lying among a cluster of lemming holes, a dark brown object which, on closer inspection, turned out to be the complete sole of a boot. Though in itself an interesting find, he soon saw that there was more to the boot part. Picking it up he could see that three large screws had been driven through the sole from the inside out, and that the screw ends on the sole bottom had been sheared off. Kowal carried the artefact back to camp where the others, who had been cataloguing the collection, examined it. It was obvious that the screws were makeshift cleats that would have given the wearer a grip on ice and snow – a grip absolutely necessary when hauling a sledge over the ice.

It was this object, more than even the bleached bones of the sailors, which brought home to the four searchers the discomfort, agony, and despair the Franklin crewmen must have endured at this final stage of the disaster. The piece of

Brass screw 'cleats'

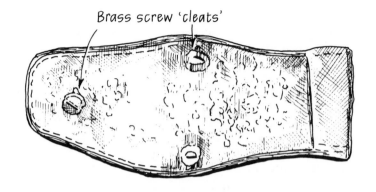

boot symbolized the final trek of the crews of the *Erebus* and *Terror*. While sitting alone during the dusk-shrouded early hours of 14 July, with brisk winds blowing in off Victoria Strait, Beattie felt that Franklin's men did indeed still watch over the place. It was as if the dead crewmen might yet rise up for one last desperate struggle to ascend the Back River to safety.

Later, Beattie, Carlson, Kowal and Tungilik surveyed 5 kilometres further to near Little Point. To the west of this location was a long inlet filled with rotten ice, effectively forming a barrier to any further survey that season. Packing their precious cargo of bones and artefacts, they readied to leave the island. With the King William Island surveys at an end, Beattie wondered what new insights into the Franklin disaster his small collection of bones would give.

Chapter Seven

A DOORWAY OPENS

During the early months of 1982, bone samples collected from the four skeletons discovered on King William Island in 1981 – three Inuit (two males, one female), and the Franklin expedition crewman from near Booth Point – were submitted to the Alberta Soil and Feed Testing Laboratory for trace element analysis.

The method of analysis used, called 'inductively coupled plasma atomic emission spectroscopy', assesses the level of a number of different elements contained in the bone. Beattie was looking for possible insights into the individuals' health and diet. At that time he believed that scurvy and starvation were the likely cause of the Franklin disaster, and the bone samples collected in 1981 were submitted without instructions to look for a particular element.

By the time Beattie returned from the field in 1982, the results of the trace element analysis were waiting for him. It was the level of lead found in the Franklin expedition crewman that immediately caught his eye. The difference between the lead levels found in the Inuit skeletons and that of the Franklin crewman was astounding. In the three Inuit skeletons the levels ranged from 22 to 36 parts per million. Such levels fall within the range identified in other human skeletons from cultures with no exposure to lead beyond that found in the environmental background. In contrast to the Inuit skeletons, the occipital bone from the Franklin crewman registered levels of 228 parts per million.

If the crewman suffered this level of intake during the course of the expedition it would have resulted in lead poisoning. The effects of lead poisoning in humans has been well documented and include a number of physical and neurological problems that can occur separately or in any combination depending on the individual and the amount absorbed. Anorexia, weakness and fatigue, irritability, stupor, paranoia, abdominal pain, and anaemia are just a few of the possible effects.

The unexpected discovery of elevated bone lead levels left Beattie struggling to understand what could have been the cause. One suspicion related to the relatively new technology of preserving foods in tin containers used by the Franklin expedition. Nearly 8,000 lead-soldered tins containing 15,100 kilograms of preserved meat were supplied to the expedition, as well as the tinned equivalent of 11,628 litres of soup, 546 kilograms of tinned pemmican and 4,037 kilograms of tinned preserved vegetables. The seams and seals of some tins are known to be a significant source of lead contamination even today, so this certainly could have been a problem. In addition, lead-glazed pottery and tableware were used by nineteenth-century British arctic expeditions. The storage and serving of acidic foods and beverages (which can dissolve lead salts), such as lemon juice, wine, vinegar or pickles, in lead-glazed vessels could have been a major source of lead ingestion during the expedition.

Other possible sources of lead included tea, chocolate and other food stored in containers lined with lead foil. In addition, food colouring, tobacco products, pewterware, and even lead-wicked candles could have added to the possible contamination.

Beattie believed that the problems of lead poisoning, compounded by the severe effects of scurvy, could have amounted to a lethal combination for many members of the expedition's crew during the early months of 1848. Rapidly declining health might well have been the major reason for the decision by Crozier and Fitzjames to desert the ships. As the note discovered by Hobson on King William Island had revealed, nine officers and fifteen men had already died by 25 April 1848.

Beattie realized that this radical new theory would prompt debate among historians, who had for so long relied on the theories of the nineteenth-century searchers and later parliamentary inquiries in Britain as the basis of their investigations. While these sources are invaluable in the reconstruction of events, all the volumes written about the doomed expedition combined were not able to provide the insights Beattie had already gained from the scanty physical remains found on King William Island.

The problem with the theory was that skeletal remains alone were not enough to make a convincing case. Although the lead values were undeniably high, bone does not reflect recent exposure so much as it does lifetime exposure. The lead sources present in the early industrial environment of mid-nineteenth-century England could have been to blame rather than any short-term exposure on the expedition. Contamination over the twenty-five or so years of the unknown Franklin crewman's life could have caused physical or neurological symptoms, but they would have been much milder than those associated with classic lead poisoning and might have resulted in only slight behavioural problems. To establish or disprove lead as a health problem on the expedition required the analysis of preserved soft tissue which would reflect lead exposure following the departure of the expedition from England in May 1845.

The unexpected discovery of high lead levels took Beattie's mind away from his just completed 1982 survey of King William Island, where the fragmentary and incomplete discoveries, albeit interesting, were nevertheless disappointing. Skeletal remains collected in 1982 would back up the bone lead findings, and provide additional proof of scurvy among the crewmen, but even a physical anthropologist could learn little more from them. Beattie instead began to look elsewhere. He looked to the only known location where Franklin crewmen died and were known to have been buried in the frozen ground by their shipmates. That place was tiny Beechey Island off the south-west coast of Devon Island.

Three sailors, Petty Officer John Torrington, Able Seaman John Hartnell and Private William Braine of the Royal Marines, had died during the first winter of the Franklin expedition and were buried in the permanently frozen ground. Beattie wondered, what if those bodies remained frozen to this time? Wouldn't they hold the key to whether his theory was true or false?

Mummified humans have given researchers and historians untold insights into life in very different worlds from our own. They are time capsules of the history and evolution of human beings. The mummified pharaohs of ancient Egypt have added greatly to our knowledge of that distant time, just as the bog people of northern Europe have shed new light on Iron Age man. But bodies have also remained frozen through great lengths of time; examples include Charles Francis Hall who died in 1871 and whose partially preserved remains were uncovered in Greenland's permafrost in 1968. Prehistoric Inuit were found entombed in the ice near Barrow, Alaska, and in Greenland, while in the Altai Mountains of south-central Siberia 2,200-year-old Scythian tombs contained frozen and partially preserved human remains. The cold arctic temperatures on Beechey Island were right for at least the chance of similar preservation, and Beattie first officially proposed the exhumation of the three graves to Canadian authorities early in 1983.

In 1981 and 1982 he had required only an archaeology permit issued by the Prince of Wales Northern Heritage Centre of the Northwest Territories and a science permit from the Science Advisory Board of the Northwest Territories to conduct his survey for skeletal remains on King William Island. The plan to dig up the buried corpses of Beechey Island, however, was far more complicated because the site was, in effect, a graveyard and the identities of the three Franklin expedition sailors were known. Beattie had to ensure that all proper authorities were notified and approved of the planned research.

Archaeology and science permits were obtained from the Territorial government, which in turn asked Beattie to inform the British Admiralty, now part of the Ministry of Defence, and also to attempt to contact any living descendants of the three sailors. The scientific team sought, and eventually received, clearance from the Chief Medical Officer of the Northwest Territories who assessed whether there was a potential health risk involved in the exposure of remains dating to the mid-nineteenth century. Exhumation and reburial permits, issued by the Department of Vital Statistics of the

Northwest Territories, were also applied for.

Permission from the Royal Canadian Mounted Police was also required, and with their assistance Beattie notified the British Ministry of Defence of the planned excavations.

The Settlement Council of the Resolute Bay community granted permission to conduct research on the site which falls within their local jurisdiction.

Finally, in an effort to contact any descendants of the three Franklin crewmen, Beattie wrote to *The Times* asking that they print a request for descendants to contact him as soon as possible. The short article produced no response.

Because of the nature of the work on Beechey Island, and what might be contained in the graves, Beattie expanded his research team to include an archaeologist and a pathologist. At last, in August 1984, the team of scientists from the University of Alberta left Edmonton for Resolute, en route to Beechey Island. They shared the same hope: that the very cold that once worked to destroy the Franklin expedition would now help to unlock the mysteries of its destruction.

PART TWO
THE ICEMEN

And here and there a churchyard grave is found
In the cold North's unhallowed ground.

Chapter Eight

ACROSS THE PRECIPICE

It is clear that all had gone exceedingly well for Sir John Franklin during the first months of his expedition. The *Erebus* and the *Terror* had dodged through the ice of Baffin Bay in 1845 and quickly passed through Lancaster Sound, the eastern entrance to the Northwest Passage. Finding their westward progress impeded by a wall of ice in Barrow Strait, Franklin turned his ships north into the unexplored Wellington Channel for some 240 kilometres, penetrating to 77° north latitude. A second barrier of ice probably forced them to retreat along the west and south coasts of Cornwallis Island, thus identifying the land mass as an island, before they found a winter harbour at Beechey Island.

They settled into their first winter camp site doubtless filled with a sense of purpose. They had not yet found a passage, but the coming summer held every hope of success.

But first Franklin and his 128 men – most of whom were without previous polar experience – had to contend with the approaching twenty-four darkness of the bitter arctic winter and temperatures that dipped to minus 40°C and colder. They would be completely isolated from all other human beings, and beyond any hope of rescue for many months should something go wrong; and then came the deaths of John Torrington, John Hartnell and William Braine.

Speculation about the cause of death of those three men dominated Owen Beattie's thoughts, when, on 10 August 1984, he and a scientific team consisting of pathologist Dr Roger Amy and research assistant Walt Kowal, Joelee Nungaq, and Geraldine Ruszala lifted off in their Twin Otter from

Resolute and turned eastward for the flight across the choppy waters of Wellington Channel to Beechey Island.

As the aircraft approached the distant cliffs of Beechey Island and nearby Devon Island, there was little to provide a sense of scale. But as the plane descended, rounding the northern spit of Beechey Island, then closed in on the sloping area of Franklin's winter camp, Beattie was astonished at how insignificant it looked alongside massive Devon Island.

He had never visited the historic site before and, peering out of the window as the plane passed by the graves at about 30 metres above the ground, he was deeply moved by its vulnerability. Along the whole eastern slope of the island the headboards of John Torrington, John Hartnell and William Braine were the tallest features visible, framed by towering, vertical cliffs to the west and the shore of Erebus Bay to the east.

Adjacent to the graves was a landing area, scored by long parallel wheel marks in the gravel, where other planes had landed, some perhaps earlier that summer, others many years earlier. The pilot, flying by the graves, checked out the makeshift landing strip and the wind direction. He then powered the Twin Otter up and out over Erebus Bay, turned sharply towards the cliffs and, pulling out of the turn, lined up with the landing area. Skimming only a metre or two over higher mounds of gravel, the plane, flaps now fully extended, was committed to a short field landing. With the graves directly off the left wing, the main wheels touched down into the gravel. Immediately, the pilot brought the nose wheel down, applied brakes, and reversed thrust on the propellers. Within 60 metres the plane had come to a full stop.

After half an hour of unloading a huge pile of supplies, the team stood back and watched the plane lift off and fly out over Union Bay, then into the distance, the droning of the engine gradually replaced by quiet. For the first few minutes the crew strolled around the site. Not a few of them were struck by feelings of absolute isolation. Apart from the Antarctic, and perhaps a handful of other places, there is nowhere in the world that a person can face solitude as in the Canadian Arctic. It is perhaps the closest experience on earth to that of the astronauts in space. Even the presence of a few workmates does not compensate for the emptiness and loneliness of the north.

The first task was to construct a temporary home, like Franklin's men had done there many years earlier. Everyone helped to pitch two large communal tents, and as soon as they were ready, five sleeping tents were set up.

The two large tents were called long-house tents. Measuring 3.7 by 5.5 metres, they provided much-needed living space for a crew whose sleeping tents were large enough only for a sleeping bag and a backpack. The long-house tents had a strong tubular aluminium skeleton which was covered by a canvas outer skin. Another canvas cover was tied on the inside, and both layers provided excellent protection from the wind, rain, and snow. A heavy canvas floor covered the sharp gravel, and the door, located at one end, consisted of a double flap that could be tied tightly shut. When all the tents were in position, the radio aerial and a weather station were assembled and raised.

Beattie spent time that first day on Beechey Island studying the tiny Franklin graveyard where he hoped some answers lay buried. The three graves lay side by side at about 8 metres above sea level. He planned to begin by exhuming Petty Officer John Torrington, who was probably the first to die on the expedition. Interred right alongside Torrington were Able-bodied Seaman John Hartnell and Private William Braine.

Torrington's headboard was simple, but both Hartnell and Braine had inscriptions taken from the Bible carved on theirs. Hartnell's included the following passage:' "Thus saith the Lord of Hosts, consider your ways." Haggai, i,7.', while Braine's read, ' "Choose ye this day whom ye will serve" Joshua, xxiv,15.' Such unusual inscriptions prompted some searchers and historians to believe foul play or mishap had marred that first winter. One of the jobs of a forensic anthropologist is to interpret whether foul play could have caused or contributed to the death of an individual, and before the work started on Torrington's grave, Beattie wondered what he might find.

Two days after the first members of Beattie's scientific team arrived, a second Twin Otter flew in carrying project archaeologist Eric Damkjar and research assistant Arne Carlson. Damkjar brought news of a family emergency to Nungaq, and the young assistant was forced to leave on the same aircraft they had arrived in.

Torrington's grave was carefully staked out, mapped, sketched and photographed so it could be returned to its original state upon completion of the exhumation. Each stone covering the grave, from the tiny (5-10 cm high) stone fence made of limestone shingle that surrounded it to the stones that covered the burial mound itself, were numbered with water-soluble ink to assist the scientists in reconstruction.

They worked surrounded by the permanence of the stark and seemingly ancient land. But for the lonesome graves, a few remaining Franklin relics, and their own small cluster of tents, there was nothing human in the place. The hard, angular coastline of Devon Island juts out in the distance east of Beechey Island, with cliffs rising two hundred or more metres out of Lancaster Sound and Barrow Strait. When the land is covered with snow the stratigraphy of the cliffs produces marked horizontal stripes of white and grey that appear like a chart of the ages. Beechey Island itself is a very small attachment to the south-west corner of Devon Island, to which it is connected by a narrow filament of gravel barely 4 metres across in parts and within the reach of wind-blown ice.

Beechey Island was first seen by Europeans on a cold August day in 1819. Captain William Edward Parry briefly described landing on Devon Island:

> The first party landed at the foot of a bluff headland, which forms the eastern point of this bay, and which I named after my friend MR RICHARD RILEY, of the Admiralty.

It was on that point of land, Cape Riley, that searchers would find the first traces of the Franklin expedition thirty-one years later. Then Parry looked to the west, across a bay that now bears the name of Franklin's ship *Erebus*, at what would eventually become one of the most important and recognized sites in arctic exploration:

. . . on the side of the bay, opposite to Cape Riley, was an island; to which I . . . gave the name of BEECHEY ISLAND, out of respect to SIR WILLIAM BEECHEY.

Parry didn't set foot on the tiny island he named.

The north-east corner of Beechey Island slopes first gently upwards from the shore of Erebus Bay through a series of level beach ridges ideal for the construction of small buildings, or a graveyard. Upslope from the area used by Franklin and his crews, the land rises more steeply, culminating in high cliffs which overlook the camp site and the bay where the two ships would have been locked in the ice. The top of the island is remarkably flat, and in the south-west corner of the plateau, overlooking Barrow Strait, Franklin had the large rock cairn built. From this vantage point, 180 metres above sea level, it is possible to see Somerset Island 70 kilometres to the south, and Cornwallis Island is easily visible 50 kilometres west across the entrance to Wellington Channel.

A small stream cuts down to south of Franklin's camp area past the grey gravel covering the three graves before emptying into Erebus Bay. Only in July and August does the stream come to life, providing a source of water for visitors to the site. In July when the sun has warmed the rocky ground, hardy flowers bloom, filling the landscape with tiny, random pockets of bright colour. But there are no trees on Beechey Island, which is far beyond the northernmost limit where trees can grow, and in August as the scientific team worked, the blooms had already fallen away.

On 12 August 1984, having erected a tent shell over the grave to protect it from the elements, the University of Alberta researchers began to dig through the ground to Torrington's grave.

It took less than an hour for the crew to remove the top layer of gravel using shovels and trowels, but when the excavation reached 10 centimetres into the ground they encountered cement-like permafrost. After a short unsuccessful experiment in melting the permafrost with hot air, they resorted to pick and shovel to attack the permanently frozen ground.

Soon after the uppermost levels of the permafrost had been

chipped, broken, and shovelled away, a strange smell was detected in the otherwise crisp and clean air. At first it wafted upwards intermittently, mingling with the smell from the smashing, sparking contact of pick with gravel, but as the excavation deepened the smell gained in strength and persistence and soon dominated the work. Though not totally a smell of decay, it served to remind Beattie of what he might encounter. Not until much later, when the coffin was fully exposed, was the origin of the smell determined.

Two long days were spent struggling through almost 1.5 metres of permafrost before the researchers got their first glimpse of the past. At the deepest part of the excavation, field assistant Walt Kowal, carefully clearing off a thin layer of snow at the foot end of the grave, exposed a small area of clear ice. Beneath the ice casing he could see dark blue material. Until this discovery, there was speculation as to whether anyone was buried there at all. Torrington's body might have plunged through the ice into the freezing waters and been lost. Other expeditions of the period had constructed dummy graves as a form of memorial. Or maybe the body would be simply missing, removed sometime during the past 138 years. The possibility originated in exasperation at about half a metre below the top of the permafrost, but as the researchers struggled deeper and deeper into the ground, and still found no sign of a coffin, the thought that the grave was empty began to trouble them. So when Kowal saw the blue material he shouted, 'That's it! We've got it!' and stood back with a sense of accomplishment and relief.

Beattie and the others quickly gathered and knelt in a close circle round the discovery. With such a small area exposed it was impossible to determine what the fabric represented. Beattie thought it might be a section of the Union Jack. Others speculated it might be part of a uniform, a shroud, or the coffin itself. For a time the material was left under the thin cover of ice.

Although the researchers had obviously discovered something in the grave and were anxious to continue, Beattie was still awaiting the exhumation and reburial permits from the government of the Northwest Territories, notification of permission from the Royal Canadian Mounted Police and clearance from the Chief Medical Officer. What had been done up to that point was considered archaeological work, and was covered by a separate permit. Having established the exact location of the body, he was forced to call an end to the excavation until the required permissions arrived.

Abundantly clear to Beattie, after removing over a metre of permafrost, was that Torrington's preservation would probably be excellent because of the ice. Originally there had been some doubts, as 138 Arctic springs and summers had passed. But even at the height of summer the season's heat had little or no effect on the upper reach of the permafrost – and Franklin's men had gone to a good deal of trouble interring Torrington deep in the frozen ground.

As the researchers waited for the permits, they were confronted with a problem that could have ruined the whole project. Water began to flood the grave.

This water was subsurface run-off from the melting snow and permafrost of the slope and cliffs inland from the excavation, and was further fed by periods of rain and sleet. Everything was at stake. What had lain undisturbed for more than a century could be severely damaged or destroyed by water within hours if they didn't act quickly.

It was decided that a shallow v-shaped ditch 40 metres long would be dug directly upslope of the graves (the three crewmen were buried alongside one another, with Torrington closest to the sea). This ditch, shovelled and scraped only a few centimetres into the permafrost, acted as a collecting canal, effectively directing the water away from the graves. Within a matter of hours the water seeping into Torrington's grave had slowed to a trickle and eventually stopped.

With still no news about the required permits, Roger Amy and Geraldine Ruszala made use of the time to explore the spit of land connecting Beechey Island to Devon Island. Well into their hike, Amy, casting his eye along the spit, noticed a dirty-coloured snow bank about one-third of a kilometre away. His eyes were drawn by its unusual colour, but as he looked more closely, he saw it move. Amy stopped dead in his tracks the second the realization hit him: they were walking directly into the path of a polar bear. These huge and powerful animals, which can weigh 900 kilograms and stand 3.5 metres on their hind legs, often avoid human contact. However, periodic polar bear attacks do take place in the Canadian Arctic, and they occur frequently enough to result in occasional bear killings by people in self-defence.

Amy whispered to Ruszala to start backing up slowly as the bear began to saunter towards them. They were at least half a kilometre from camp, and they continued this cautious retreat almost the whole distance, with the bear following along at the same speed. Finally, with the camp within earshot, they turned and ran. 'A bear, a bear,' Ruszala shouted, wildly pointing back towards the spit. The bear was still about a third of a kilometre away when Kowal and Damkjar fired several shots into the air to frighten the animal. These first blasts simply increased the bear's curiosity, but the two men continued firing and after ambling a few metres closer, the bear wisely decided it might be better, if not simply quieter, to alter its direction and move on to other business. The crew followed the majestic animal's retreat until it was last seen swimming speedily across Union Bay towards Cape Spencer. Amy and Ruszala, however, appeared badly shaken by the experience of being stalked.

As the wait for the final permits continued, Beattie and Damkjar decided to explore first the remains of Franklin's winter camp and then historic sites along the east coast of the island.

Most of the relics left behind by Franklin's expedition were collected and taken away by the search expeditions that followed. What remained was subjected to continual disturbance right up to 1984. Despite this, a number of important features remained in the areas adjacent to the graveyard. Most prominent among them was a large gravel-walled outline believed to have been a storehouse. Also nearby the graves was all that remained of a smithy, a carpenter's shop, and, further away, depressions where tent structures or observation platforms once stood. Between 1976 and 1982, Parks Canada conducted detailed archaeological investigations of a number of important historical sites in the Arctic. Beechey Island was one of the sites studied, and the only artefacts from Franklin's expedition remaining at that time – besides the structure outlines – were clay pipe fragments, nails, forge waste, a stove door fragment, wood shavings and tin cans.

Beattie also looked over two graves dating from the searches of the 1850s which had been dug alongside Torrington, Hartnell and Braine. One of the graves belongs to Thomas Morgan, a seaman from Robert McClure's ship HMS *Investigator*. The origin of the other is less certain, although one journal from the 1850s indicates it may be a dummy grave serving as a memorial to French Navy Lieutenant Joseph Réné Bellot.

Both had died heroic and tragic deaths. Morgan had been among the scurvy-wracked men from the *Investigator* who – before the Franklin expedition achievements were discovered – had been credited with being the first to cross the Northwest Passage. Having abandoned the ice-locked *Investigator* with the rest of McClure's crew at Mercy Bay on the north coast of Banks Island, Morgan had made the difficult trek by foot over the ice first to Dealy Island, then later reached Beechey Island, only to die aged thirty-six on 22 May 1854 on board HMS *North Star*. Bellot, who had served in the French Navy with distinction, later volunteered to join in the Franklin search. Bellot visited the Arctic first under Captain William Kennedy aboard the *Prince Albert*, then later aboard HMS *Phoenix*. On 18 August 1853, while carrying dispatches to searcher Sir Edward Belcher up icy Wellington Channel, Bellot was caught by a gust of wind and swept into the frigid water. His body was never recovered.

Beattie and Damkjar, leaving the graves and adjacent Franklin camp site behind them, walked south along the beach ridge above the water line. The first artefacts found along their route were tins, scattered individually, or in small clusters. Close inspection of the cans identified them as being from the supplies of the search expeditions. Not only had Captain Horatio Thomas Austin and Captain William Penny – the searchers who had first discovered Franklin expedition relics at Beechey Island – spent time there, but others later used the island as a base for their searches. Walking along, the number of tins increased, and wood fragments also became evident.

Visible around a curve in the coastline was the mast of one of several vessels left at King William Island during the 1850s. The mast was jutting at a steep angle out of a gravel beach ridge. The vessel, which was probably left on the island to serve as a depot, was still largely intact in 1927 when Sir Frederick Banting, co-discoverer of insulin, and Canadian painter A.Y. Jackson visited the island on a sketching trip. The mast, and a small section from the hull of the vessel which lay flat on one of the lower beach ridges, were all that remained for Beattie and Damkjar to inspect.

Other features along the coastline soon came into view. Along one of the highest beach ridges were a series of recent markers and cairns dating from the 1950s to the 1970s. Also at the site stands a memorial combining the monument left by Leopold M'Clintock in 1858 and a cenotaph erected by Belcher as a memorial to all those who had died during the Franklin search.

Belcher, commanding a British naval fleet of five ships from 1852 to 1854, ordered one of the ships, the *North Star* under the command of William John Samuel Pullen, to remain off Beechey Island as a base for the other vessels. Directly in front of the cenotaph, and on a much lower ridge, is the skeleton of Northumberland House, the supply depot built by the crew of the *North Star* in 1854. It had been in a reasonable and useful state of repair even earlier this century, but no longer. Only parts of the wood walls were still visible, and a stone wall had held up quite well. Scattered in and around the structure were hundreds, possibly thousands, of artefacts from the structure itself and from the food containers (primarily wooden barrel staves and metal barrel hoops) that were once housed inside. On 6 August 1927 when Banting and Jackson visited Northumberland House, significant damage had already been done to the structure, although Jackson noted in his journal that 'there are a lot of water barrels, thirty or forty of them, that could be used today'.

The scattered relics on Beechey Island do not attest to the hundreds of men from various expeditions who spent time at the site over the course of the searches of the early 1850s. Even on such a small island the remains are lost among the forbidding landscape.

Looking off the south shore of the island during his explorations, Beattie thought of the wreck of the *Breadalbane*, sent from England with fresh supplies for the ships under Belcher. Crushed in the ice, the *Breadalbane* sank off the island on 21 August 1853. In 1980, Canadian underwater explorer Dr Joe MacInnis located the remains of the remarkably preserved ship under 100 metres of water and in 1983 led a diving team to visit the wreck.

Returning to camp from his hike, Beattie saw that the wait for permissions was taking its toll on everyone's nerves, and finally Amy, feeling that these permissions would not be granted in time to complete the project that summer, decided to return to Edmonton, where he had a number of pressing professional obligations. Amy left Beechey Island on 15 August.

At last, on 17 August Beattie received a radio transmission from the Polar Shelf offices in Resolute giving permission to proceed with the exhumation, autopsy, and reburial of John Torrington. Hearing the letters of permission read over the radio caused a great sense of relief, as well as a new surge of energy and enthusiasm. The last letter graphically detailed the

HMS *Breadalbane* (left) and *Phoenix* landing provisions at Cape Riley

procedures to follow should contagious disease be detected in the Franklin crewmen. This caused some embarrassment. Everyone in the Arctic could have picked up the transmission and heard the Polar Shelf radio operator read in part: 'If in the course of the excavations Dr Beattie discovers any evidence of infectious disease in the artefacts or corpses exhumed, further digging should be discontinued.'

Work on clearing off the last layer of ice and gravel began almost immediately, and the source of the noxious odour became apparent. It was not partly decomposed tissue as had been expected but rather the rotting blue wool fabric which covered the coffin.

As they neared the coffin lid, the wind picked up dramatically and a massive, black thunder cloud moved over the site. The walls of the tent covering the excavation began to snap loudly, and as the weather continued to worsen the five researchers finally stopped their work and looked at one another. The conditions had suddenly become so strange that Kowal observed, 'This is like something out of a horror film'. Some of the crew were visibly nervous and Beattie decided to call a halt to work for the day. That night the wind howled continuously, rattling the sides of Beattie's tent all night and sometimes smacking its folds against his face, making sleep difficult. Ruszala, unable to sleep, stayed in one of the long-house tents. All were concerned about the stability of the tent that had been erected over Torrington's grave, and through the night anxious heads would peer out of their tents to check on it.

Towards morning a violent gust slashed its way under the floorless tent, lifting it up and over the headboard, before slamming it down on the adjacent beach ridge. Only a single rope held to its metal stake, preventing the tent from blowing into Erebus Bay. In the morning the weather finally calmed and they dismantled the tent, remarkably only slightly damaged, and continued their excavation in the open.

Time was not a major consideration during the work, and with continuous daylight, all soon lost track of the actual time of day. Eating when hungry, sleeping when tired, a natural rhythm developed, resulting in a work 'day' stretching up to twenty-eight hours in length. The only reminders of the regimented, time-oriented outside world were the daily 7 a.m. and 7 p.m. radio schedules with the Polar Shelf operators. During these broadcasts they would pass along weather information and messages, and listen to the messages and weather reported in turn from the other Polar Shelf-supported camps strewn across the Arctic.

As the last layer of ice and gravel cemented to the top of the coffin was removed, Damkjar thought he could see something different in the texture of the fabric on the upper central portion of the lid. 'Look at this,' he said, while continuing the thawing and cleaning. 'It looks like something is attached to the lid, or maybe carved into it'. Damkjar's slow and meticulous work seemed to take ages, but at last the discovery began to take form. It was a beautiful hand-painted plaque that had been securely nailed to the coffin lid.

The plaque was roughly heart-shaped, with short, pointed extensions along its top and bottom edges. It was made of tinned wrought iron, perhaps part of a tin can, and looked as though it was hand cut. It was painted dark blue-green, and on it in white was a carefully hand-painted inscription: 'John Torrington died January 1st, 1846, aged 20 years'.

The plaque was a touching last gesture made by Torrington's shipmates, and Damkjar spent a lot of time studying and sketching the discovery. Frozen for 138 years, the paint was showing signs of peeling, and rust had accumulated around its outer edges. The rust was carefully cleaned away, and the plaque's surface lightly brushed with water to remove the accumulated crust of silt.

The coffin itself was impressive. It was obviously well made and its mahogany lid and box had been individually covered by wool fabric dyed dark blue. White linen tape had been tacked to the lid and box in a geometric, military, yet decorative manner which contrasted with the personal nature of the plaque. Bolted to the sides of the coffin were brass handles, the one on the right still in the 'up' position, and bolted to the foot and head ends were brass rings.

What was most remarkable was the size of the coffin – it appeared almost too small to contain an adult, though this may have been an optical illusion created by the box being in a narrow hole.

During the hours spent removing the permafrost adhering to the coffin the researchers would occasionally tap on the lid, expecting to hear a hollow sound each time, but this was not the case. Rather, it was like striking a large block of marble, a strange sound given the circumstances. It obviously represented a heavy mass. It couldn't be just a body.

The removal of the lid was surprisingly difficult. It was very strongly secured to the box by a series of square shafted nails, and, as the researchers were soon to find out, it was 'glued' down by ice within the coffin. The options for removing the lid were to pry it up, pull the nails, or shear the nails at the junction of the lid with the box. Prying the lid would have almost certainly destroyed it: the wood was soft and delicate. For a similar reason they decided not to attempt to pull the nails out of the coffin. The best method, in Beattie's mind, was to shear the nails. He placed the chisel edge of a rock hammer against the lid/box junction at each nail location and struck the rock hammer inward with another hammer. The chisel head drove into and through the nail without damage to the coffin.

Finally, after all the nails had been sheared and the ice holding down the lid had thawed, Beattie took the foot end and slowly lifted it up, revealing the shadowy contents of the coffin. A partially transparent block of ice lay within, and through the frozen bubbles, cracks and planes in the ice, something could be seen. But the more closely they looked, the more elusive it became.

This block of ice was the most serious obstacle yet. They had come to within centimetres of reaching the body, only to be confronted with an apparently insurmountable obstacle. Work stopped while Beattie brooded over the next step. The options were few.

An aircraft engine preheater on the site, a noisy, temperamental, and dangerous machine, could not be used to thaw the ice because hot air would put the biological matter and any artefacts at considerable risk. The outside air temperature was always at or slightly below freezing, and in the grave lower still, so natural thawing was not a possibility.

Chipping away the ice was not practical, and probably impossible.

Then Ruszala suggested pouring water, some heated, some cold, on the ice block. It worked better and faster than could have been hoped for. The researchers heated buckets of stream water on the camp stoves, lugged them bucket-brigade style dozens of metres to the grave, and poured the water over a selected section of ice, from where it eventually ran out of the bottom join of the coffin onto the floor of the grave. This run-off was scooped up into a pail and dumped away from the grave site. They worked hard and progress was swift, spurred on by the knowledge that they would soon come face to face with a man from the Franklin expedition.

The first part of Torrington to come into view was the front of his shirt, complete with mother-of-pearl buttons. Much more exciting, though, were his perfectly preserved toes which gradually poked through the receding ice.

Most of the day was spent at this initial stage of exposure. The face remained shielded, covered by a fold of the same blue wool that had lain over the outside of the coffin. This created an eerie feeling among the researchers; it was almost as if Torrington was somehow aware of what was happening around him.

It would not be long before they were to gaze upon the face of this man from history. And, but for artists' portraits, and a few primitive photographs from the period, who living today has ever seen the face of a person from the earlier part of the last century, a person who had taken part in one of history's major expeditions of discovery?

Beattie was fascinated by the almost perfect preservation of the toes. However, in concentrating so long on the feet, the realization that a completely preserved human was attached to them had not yet sunk in. This was a strange period during their work: they were extremely close to a frozen sailor from 1846, and yet were concentrating so much on small details of thawing that the eventual exposure of the complete person was totally unexpected.

While Beattie worked on the feet, Arne Carlson was painstakingly thawing the section of coffin fabric covering the face area. Using a pair of large surgical tweezers he pulled the material up carefully as it was freed by the melting ice. This was a very difficult and meticulous task as he tried to prevent any tearing of the material and had to work hunched closely to it. Then suddenly, as he pulled gently upward on the right edge of the material, the last curtain of ice gave way, freeing the material and revealing the face of John Torrington. Carlson gasped and sprang to his feet, allowing the fabric to fall back on Torrington's face. Pointing with the tweezers, Carlson said in a strangely calm voice: 'He's there, he's right there!' The others quickly gathered at the graveside and while everyone peered at the fabric covering, Beattie seized its edge and pulled it back.

All stood numbed and silent. Nothing could have prepared them for the face of John Torrington, framed and cradled in his ice-coffin. Despite all the intervening years, the young man's life did not seem far away; in many ways it was as if Torrington had just died.

It was a shattering moment for Beattie, who felt an empathy for this man and a sadness for his passing, and who also felt as if he were standing at a precipice looking across a terrifying gulf at a very different world from our own.

The sky on the day of the autopsy was overcast, grey clouds merging with the grey waters of Erebus Bay. The temperature was -1°C, and the wind was a steady 20 kilometres per hour from the south. Standing at the graveside and looking into the coffin, the gloom seemed to be reflected in Torrington's simple grey linen trousers and his shirt, white with closely spaced thin blue stripes. The shirt had a high collar, and the waist downwards, tucked into the trousers, was pleated. Around his chin and over the top of his medium-brown hair was tied his kerchief, made of white cotton and covered in large blue polka-dots.

John Torrington looked anything but grotesque. The expression on his thin face, with the pouting mouth and the half-closed eyes gazing through delicate, light-brown eyelashes, was peaceful. His nose and forehead, in contrast to the natural skin colour of the rest of his face, were darkened by contact with the blue wool coffin covering. This shadowed the face, accentuating the softness of its appearance. The tragedy of

Torrington's young death was as apparent to the researchers then as it must have been to his shipmates 138 years before.

Torrington would have stood 163 centimetres (5 feet 4 inches) tall. His arms were straight, with the hands resting palm down on the fronts of his thighs, and held in position by strips of cotton binding. These bindings were located at his elbows, hands, ankles and his big toes. Their purpose was to hold the limbs together during the preparation of the body for burial. It was discovered later that his body lay on a bed of wood shavings scattered along the bottom of the coffin, with his head supported by a thicker matting of shavings. He wore no shoes or boots, and there were no other personal belongings beyond his clothing.

By far the strongest and most vivid memory Beattie has of that summer centres around the final thawing of Torrington's body in the coffin and lifting him out of the grave in preparation for an autopsy.

It was a remarkable and highly emotional experience, with Carlson holding and supporting his legs, Beattie his shoulders and head. He was very light, weighing less than 40 kilograms (6 stone) and as they moved him his head rolled onto Beattie's left shoulder; Beattie looked directly into Torrington's half-opened eyes, only a few centimetres from his own. He was not stiff like a dead man, and though his arms and legs were bound, he was limp. 'It's as if he's just unconscious,' Beattie said.

The two men carefully lowered Torrington to the ground outside the grave. There he lay, open to the arctic sky which he had left behind 138 years before. If he had miraculously stirred to consciousness after this long sleep, Torrington would have thought that he had missed just two changes of season – a sleep of but eight months.

The bindings were removed and the body undressed. Away from the reality of the research project, an observer could suggest that the undressing of the body was an indignity to Torrington. But in their situation, both with the need for medical evidence on the fate of Franklin's expedition, and their own feelings which were very personal and intense, no indignity could exist.

Looking at Torrington lying naked on the autopsy tarpaulin,

Beattie saw for the first time the emaciated condition of the young sailor and was shocked by the appearance of the body. All wondered aloud at what could have been the cause. Had he died of starvation? Was he suffering from some serious disease which had robbed him of his physical strength? It was immediately evident that foul play was unlikely; what they saw was a young man who was extremely ill when he died.

Torrington's emaciated appearance was to a small extent due to the loss of moisture which occurs over a prolonged period of freezing, and in that sense preservation could not be described as perfect. But every rib in his body was visible and later, during the autopsy, no fat could be found, confirming that the weight loss before death was real and significant.

His hands, which Beattie commented 'look like they are still warm', were extremely long, delicate and smooth, 'like you would expect a pianist's to be'. There were no calluses on the palms or fingers, features to be expected on an active participant in the expedition. Torrington had been the leading stoker on the *Terror*, and it would be normal for his hands to show some evidence of his work if he had been recently active. There was none, and for that reason Beattie was convinced he must have been too ill to work for some time before he died. Also, his nails were quite clean and he had recently been given a haircut, either in preparation for his burial or perhaps in the period just before his death.

The first part of the examination was a meticulous search for external signs of the cause or causes of death (wounds, markings, disease), or of medical treatment (signs of medicinal bleeding). None was found except for deep and discoloured marks on the elbows, hands, and ankles made by the cotton bindings. Then Beattie conducted a standard autopsy. Tissue, organ, bone, fingernail, and hair samples were taken for analysis by Roger Amy at his laboratory at the University of Alberta.

The autopsy took more than four hours to complete. Beattie and Carlson wore surgical aprons, and their hands were double gloved with rubber surgical gloves. The procedure involved making a Y-shaped incision in the chest and abdomen, retracting the skin and musculature, the temporary removal of the front portion of the rib cage and exposure of the thoracic and abdominal organs. When the autopsy began, all internal structures were completely frozen. It was necessary to thaw each organ with water before samples could be collected. Using a scalpel, 10-20 grams of tissue were collected from each organ. Carlson and Damkjar prepared and marked the sample containers with identification information and numbers. A preservative was poured in them, and Beattie dropped each collected sample in the appropriate container, which was then sealed. Damkjar also took pictures of the various stages of the autopsy, while Kowal took notes dictated to him by Beattie. One of the most difficult aspects of the whole procedure was keeping their hands warm, and one bucket of hot water was kept nearby so that Beattie and Carlson could immerse their hands to warm them up.

From the beginning Beattie could see features which could be of medical importance. The lungs, when exposed, appeared completely blackened, and they were attached abnormally in a number of locations to the chest wall by a series of adhesions (scar tissue). Torrington's heart also appeared abnormal. No food could be found in the stomach or bowel.

Torrington's right thumbnail was collected, as were samples of his hair, rib bone, and radius bone. These would be subjected to various forms of analysis in later months in an attempt to construct a diary of his health during the time he spent on the expedition prior to his death, as well as some short period of time prior to the expedition.

A difficult but necessary procedure during an autopsy is the exposure of the brain. With a surgical hand saw, and with assistance from Carlson and Damkjar, Beattie removed the skull cap and collected samples of brain tissue and made observations of the brain anatomy. All of the samples collected and observations made would be pieced together later after Amy's analysis of the data and microscopic evidence from the samples.

During the autopsy Beattie saw that, even though the preservation was excellent, post-mortem degenerative changes in the structure of the tissues had taken place. Amy would confirm later that the microscopic detail showed virtually all cellular structures were badly or completely damaged. The brain had shrunk, as had some of the other organs, to about two-thirds of its normal size, and had completely autolyzed (the cells had been destroyed by their own enzymes). Later, Beattie would be approached a number of times by people with the idea that perhaps one day in the future Torrington could have been revived, but the evidence of massive cellular damage found in every organ precluded this possibility.

Beattie kept Torrington's face covered throughout the autopsy; somehow, this gave the reassurance that his privacy was maintained and illustrated how strongly the face is perceived as the window of the soul and the reflection of our identity.

After the autopsy Torrington was re-dressed, lifted back into his grave, and into the coffin. After carefully positioning his body, the lid was then replaced. Water would soon begin to fill the grave again, and freeze, ensuring Torrington's lasting preservation.

Ruszala had placed a note in the grave giving the names of the seven researchers and a description of their feelings and purpose at the site. It was a private offering to John Torrington which, along with his body, will quite likely outlast all of our own physical remains.

The group quietly gathered together, Ruszala suggesting it was time for silent prayer and some individual thoughts before John Torrington was again assigned to the frozen depths, maybe this time for ever. For those moments Beattie contemplated Torrington's life and the events of late 1845 and early 1846, and his own in the summer of 1984, and how the years separating the two had somehow vanished.

After filling in the grave he stopped to peer down the beach towards Erebus Bay. It was almost possible to see the two ships held in the ice just offshore, Franklin's men moving ghost-like in small groups on the ice and across the island.

The crews would have paused for John Torrington on those bitter January days of 1846, but none could have guessed what horror his death foretold. Their adventure was young and the Northwest Passage, which had haunted men for 300 years, beckoned somewhere across the icy waters to the west.

Chapter Nine

THE FACE OF DEATH

The arctic summer of 1984 was nearing an end. Though the weather had been generally good, except for the occasional light dusting of snow, the warmth of the summer sun was lost towards the end of August and the nights became cold. As each day brought winter closer, nightfall too gradually crept into the twenty-four-hour light of the arctic summer, and a generator had to be used to power a photoflood lamp inside the cook tent during the evenings.

The weather became so unpredictable that, if the team had radioed for an airplane from Resolute to come and pick them up, the half-hour required to fly the distance could have seen a complete change in weather. And a simple change in wind direction or a quickly dropping cloud ceiling would have made a landing at Beechey Island impossible.

Beattie had originally hoped to uncover all three of the Franklin expedition graves on the island that summer but, worried about the weather and drained by the experience of exhuming John Torrington, his thoughts began to turn towards the laboratory work that awaited him in Edmonton.

Three days had been spent on Torrington's final exhumation and autopsy and the scientific team was exhausted, physically and emotionally. Beattie wanted to pack it in for the season, as did the others. Just one radio call to the Polar Shelf and they could be away from the island. But something had bothered Beattie and the others about the appearance of Hartnell's grave, and, before completing the autopsy on John Torrington, Walt Kowal had begun to dig into the permafrost covering John Hartnell.

111

A close inspection of the graves of John Hartnell and William Braine showed that their construction by the crew of the *Erebus* had been very similar, if not identical. But they were no longer so: it was clear that Hartnell's grave had been disturbed sometime in the 138 years since his death. The large limestone slabs, at one time part of a grave structure like Braine's, which had an almost crypt-like appearance, had been simply piled on top of the burial place, as if they had been lifted away and later hastily replaced. Inspecting the surface of the grave, and looking closely into the nooks and pockets produced by the large rocks, the researchers found small fragments of wood and some tiny scraps of blue material similar to that which covered Torrington's coffin. Beattie had no idea when the grave had been disturbed. They discussed the situation, as well as the difficulty of completing an autopsy on Hartnell within the time remaining. If there had been one or more previous openings of the grave, they would have to take great care in gathering the evidence – and the time required for this could be considerable. Beattie decided to look for clues that might explain the history of the damage and determine the state of preservation, but to conduct the autopsy another year.

Before the excavation of Hartnell's grave was complete, Beattie visited a site which would add important insights into his research. Located nearly 1 kilometre north of the grave site, and at the narrowest point of the island near the spit, is a large oval mound with a central depression filled with the fragments of hundreds of rusted and distintegrating food tins from Franklin's expedition. When this location was discovered in August 1850, searchers found a neat arrangement of 700 or more tins piled 'like shot' into low pyramids about half a metre high. The tins were empty of food and had been filled with gravel. The reason for the 'cairn', as it was described, is not clear. Not wanting to miss any possible clue left behind by Franklin's people, the searchers of 1850 thoroughly investigated each of the tins, dumping out the gravel. Literally leaving no stone unturned, they also dug into the ground underneath the tins with the hope of finding a buried document. It is this excavation that produced the oval mound and depression which marks the site today.

There has been much debate about the significance of these tins. It was thought that the 'cairn' was evidence of problems with the preserved food. Certainly, by the 1850s Stephan Goldner, who had supplied the Franklin expedition, was encountering problems with the quality of the tinned foods he delivered to later expeditions. And more than one of the searchers observed that a number of the tins at Beechey Island had bulging ends, which was evidence that some of the food had putrefied. However, one twentieth-century historian has argued that the number of tins present at the site was not in excess of what was expected to have been used by the expedition during their stay at Beechey Island. In other words, there was no evidence for bad food being dumped at Beechey Island.

Beattie had seen photographs of food tins from various British arctic expeditions, and had handled a few, but as he picked through the tins from Franklin's expedition, he saw that they were different. The lead soldering was thick and sloppily done, and had dripped like melted candle wax down the inside surface of the tins. Beattie wondered if this could be the source of the lead in the Booth Point skeleton. This idea became more credible as each piece of tin he picked up demonstrated the same degree of internal contamination from the solder. Samples were collected for further examination, and a return to the dump was planned in order for a comprehensive study to be made.

Meanwhile, Kowal was finding the excavation of Hartnell's grave much more difficult than had been experienced with Torrington. The permafrost was harder and more consolidated than was encountered in the other grave, and he constantly commented on this difference. The increased difficulty in the pick and shovel work hinted that the grave had been disturbed then refrozen. As digging continued, more fragments of wood and blue material were pulled from the grave fill itself, reinforcing Beattie's view that the previous disturbance had been considerable and may have involved the exposure of the coffin and probably Hartnell's body as well.

Shortly, Kowal announced that he had found the foot end of the coffin. To everyone's surprise it was not deeply buried, only 85 centimetres into the ground. They had expected a burial at least as deep as Torrington's.

The white tape decoration on it was in poor condition, and as Kowal continued to clear the permafrost from the top of the lid, he uncovered areas of damage. 'Someone sure did a number on this grave,' he said as he finished exposing the lid. The right-hand side at the forearm level had been smashed through, leaving a gaping hole. It was possible to identify each blow of the pickaxe which had done the damage. A large rectangular piece of the blue fabric adjacent to the hole was missing. The lid, originally nailed to the coffin, was slightly ajar, the nails having either been removed or broken. There was no doubt that the coffin had been exposed and opened before. The condition of the white fabric tape decoration was in stark contrast to the symmetrical dignity of Torrington's coffin and Beattie was shocked by the damage to the coffin which at first appeared to have been caused by a blatant act of vandalism. But as work continued it became obvious that although there had been considerable damage done during the previous excavation, it was not the work of vandals. The lid had been replaced and the nails appeared to have been carefully removed. Vandals would have simply pried the lid off the coffin, causing major structural damage.

Beattie jumped into the grave and bent over the hole in the lid. Pulling some of the gravel out of the hole, he said, 'Look at this – Hartnell's shirt!' A small piece of fabric, nearly identical in design to John Torrington's shirt, had come free from the ice. The fabric, obviously part of the right shirt sleeve, was torn, and the thought entered Beattie's mind that, if the clothing had been damaged in the area of the hole in the lid, perhaps there was damage to Hartnell's body as well.

Unlike Torrington's, there was no plaque on the lid of Hartnell's coffin, and Beattie believed the plaque was removed by the people who had exposed the coffin. A close inspection of the wood in the area where a plaque would have been fixed did not reveal any nail holes, though it is possible they could have closed since the time of the plaque's removal. A less satisfactory interpretation was that, being an able seaman, Hartnell did not warrant a plaque. Considering that his mess mates (including his elder brother Thomas) would normally have been responsible for the preparation of a plaque, it seems likely there had been one.

Not only had Hartnell been buried at only a little more than half the depth of John Torrington, the coffin did not seem to be aligned with the headboard. As the researchers intended to expose no more than the coffin lid, an assessment of damage to the rest of the coffin would have to wait until their planned return.

When Kowal lifted the coffin lid on 23 August, everyone was crouched round the graveside. Inside Hartnell's coffin there was again a solid block of ice. 'There is no doubt that he will be as well preserved as Torrington,' Beattie said. However, unspoken was a fear that Hartnell's body, as well as the coffin, had been damaged. There was only one way to confirm these fears.

John Torrington was a frail, innocent-looking young man. His was not the image of a sea-toughened sailor and adventurer, but simply of a young man who died too soon. Because of this experience with Torrington, not one of the scientists was prepared for the vision of death that awaited them a few centimetres below the ice in Hartnell's coffin.

Kowal poured water over Hartnell's face area, and soon spotted the outline of a nose through the receding ice. While John Torrington's face had been slightly discoloured by contact with the coffin covering, and by exposure to a pocket of air, Hartnell's nose appeared natural in colour. Gradually Kowal could see a ghostly image taking shape through the ice – a frightening, shimmering face of death.

'This guy is spooky,' Kowal said while continuing the exposure of Hartnell, 'the quintessential pirate. This guy is frightening'.

The others watched in silence as the face was finally completely exposed. Perhaps the emotional drain of their work with Torrington was only now taking its toll. As with Torrington they were shaken by the second face that was emerging from the rock-hard ground of the island. Shaken, but in a different way.

Whereas Torrington had embodied a youthful, tragic

innocence, John Hartnell reflected the harsh realities of death and suffering in the Arctic: his was the face of a sea-hardened nineteenth-century sailor. His right eye socket appeared empty, and his lips were rigidly pursed as if he were shouting his rage at dying so early in his adventure. John Hartnell's last thoughts and the intensity of the pain he suffered during those final moments of life had been captured on his face.

His features were tightly framed by a cap, a shroud drawn up under his red-bearded chin, and the contours of melting ice on either side. A lock of dark hair could be seen below the rim of the cap, and unlike the right side, his left eye appeared normal. 'I wonder why there is such a difference in the preservation of the eyes,' Beattie mumbled, as each took a turn to examine Hartnell. 'Was the eye injured before his death? Was it diseased?' Answers to the countless questions would have to await their planned return to Beechey Island.

Besides the face, they exposed only the clothing covering the right forearm. The body had been covered in a shroud, or sheet. A portion of the shroud and the underlying shirt sleeve of his right arm had been exposed and torn by the pickaxe used during the original exhumation. There also appeared to be damage to the arm itself. The total time of Hartnell's exposure was close to twelve hours.

Later, back in the labs and libraries of Edmonton, Beattie began to piece together a solution to the mystery of Hartnell's disturbance. Sir Edward Belcher was the first to dig into the graves in October 1852, but he was discouraged by the resistant permafrost and his men gave up after only excavating a few centimetres. A month later members of a privately funded search expedition exhumed Hartnell. Leader of the expedition was Commander Edward A. Inglefield, and he was accompanied by Dr Peter Sutherland who had suggested such an exhumation while serving with Captain William Penny's search expedition two years earlier.

Inglefield's arctic exploits were considerable and in 1853 he was awarded the Royal Geographical Society's Arctic medal. During the award speech, Sir Roderick Murchison (head of the Society) described the exhumation. The transcript of the speech reflects a number of errors and embellishments:

Right: The 150-metre cliffs directly behind the Franklin winter camp on Beechey Island

Below: The view from the top of the cliffs. The tents of the 1984 field party can be seen. The spit of land in the upper part of the photograph connects with Devon Island

The grave of 25-year-old John Hartnell

John Hartnell's coffin, damaged in 1852 when his body was exhumed by Commander Inglefield and Dr Sutherland

First view of John Hartnell

John Hartnell. He was
wrapped in a shroud, wearing
a cap which when removed
revealed a full head of
dark brown hair. The bottom
of his shirt (right) was
embroidered with the date
1844 and the initials TH,
suggesting the shirt may
have belonged to his brother
Thomas

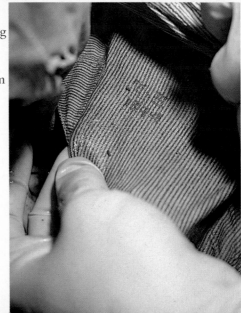

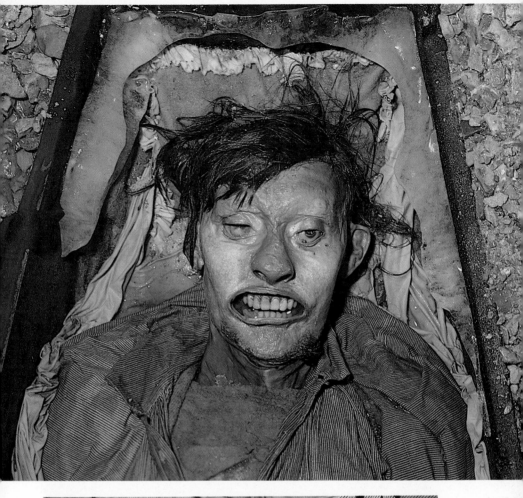

Right: Eric Damkjar inspecting the monument erected by Sir Edward Belcher to commemorate all those who died searching to discover the fate of Franklin's expedition

Below: Owen Beattie standing at the ruin of Northumberland House, the supply depot built in 1854 by the crew of the *North Star*, part of the fleet commanded by Belcher

Above: Cape Riley where
the first traces of
Franklin's expedition were
discovered

Right: A polar bear
investigates the field
party's camp

The camp illuminated by the midnight sun

Walt Kowal taking a bath

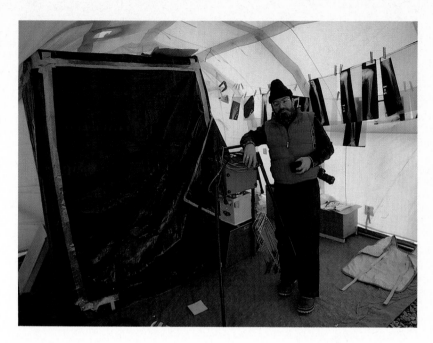

Larry Anderson in the autopsy/x-ray tent. He is leaning on the
portable x-ray unit; the black structure is a portable darkroom

Beginning the excavation of William Braine's grave. Left to right are
Walt Kowal, Arne Carlson, Jim Savelle, and Joelee Nungaq

The shrouded body of William Braine, his face covered by a red kerchief

The kerchief is drawn back to reveal Braine's face

William Braine

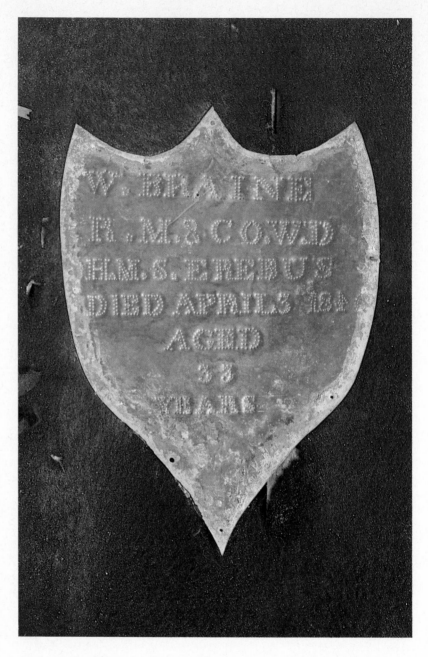

Copper plaque found nailed to William Braine's coffin lid. It reads:
'W. Braine R.M. 8 Co. W.D. Died April 3rd 1846 Aged 33 years'

. . . Commander Inglefield, being in a private expedition, resolved to dig down into the frozen ground, for the purpose of ascertaining the condition in which the men had been interred. The opening out of one coffin quite realized the object he had in view, for at six feet beneath the surface, a depth reached only with great difficulty, by penetrating frozen ground as hard as a rock, a coffin, with the name of Wm. Heartwell, was found in as perfect order as if recently deposited in the churchyard of an English village. Every button and ornament had been neatly arranged, and what was most important, the body, perfectly preserved by the intense cold, exhibited no trace of scurvy, or other malignant disease, but was manifestly that of a person who had died of consumption, a malady to which it was further known that the deceased was prone.

Inglefield's expedition was one of those supported by Lady Jane Franklin. With a crew of seventeen on board the screw schooner *Isabel* of 149 Imperial tons, they were at Beechey Island on 7 September 1852. In his published journal, Inglefield described his first sight of the graves:

That sad emblem of mortality – the grave – soon met my eye, as we plunged along through the knee-deep snow which covered the island. The last resting place of three of Franklin's people was closely examined; but nothing that had not hitherto been observed could we detect. My companion told me that a huge bear was seen continually sitting on one of the graves keeping a silent vigil over the dead.

Inglefield did not describe the exhumation of Hartnell in this journal, but there is a blank period in it covering the time between when he and Sutherland finished dining with the officers of the *North Star* and the departure of the *Isabel* from Beechey Island shortly after midnight '. . . with as beautiful a moon to light our path as ever shone on the favoured shores of our own native land'. An unpublished letter written by Inglefield to Rear-Admiral Sir Francis Beaufort on 14 September 1852, fills in this gap:

My doctor assisted me, and I have had my hand on the arm and face of poor Hartnell. He was decently clad in a cotton shirt, and though the dark night precluded our seeing, still our touch detected that a wasting illness was the cause of dissolution. It was a curious and solemn scene on the silent snow-covered sides of the famed Beechey Island, where the two of us stood at midnight. The pale moon looking down upon us as we silently worked with pickaxe and shovel at the hard-frozen tomb, each blow sending a spur of red sparks from the grave where rested the messmate of our lost countrymen. No trace but a piece of fearnought half down the coffin lid could we find. I carefully restored everything to its place and only brought away with me the plate that was nailed on the coffin lid and a scrap of the cloth with which the coffin was covered.

A remarkable letter and, as Beattie's 1984 research showed, very accurate in its description of what had happened, even down to the piece of fabric removed. This was all the evidence that was needed to explain the history of the grave's disturbance, the cause of the damage and the mystery of the missing plaque.

The location of the plaque and fabric today is unknown.

Based on Beattie's experience at the site, the actual excavation of Hartnell's grave would have taken three people nearly twenty hours to complete. It seems likely that Inglefield and Sutherland had put their crewmen to work for a good part of 7 September digging into the grave while they themselves dined and socialized with the officers of the *North Star*. There can be no doubt, when their activities of that day are plotted out, that Inglefield and Sutherland would have been at the grave site for only three or four hours prior to midnight, the appointed time for their ship the *Isabel* to set sail. As their stay at Beechey Island was so brief, and the amount of time required to excavate the grave considerable, it seems likely they had carefully planned the work prior to their arrival.

By this stage in the 1984 field season there was no hope that the medical investigations of Hartnell and William Braine could be completed. It was obvious the scientific team would have to return to the Arctic island again to complete the research.

After photographs were taken of Hartnell they began reconstructing the coffin and the grave site. The lid was replaced on the coffin in the slightly askew position in which it had been discovered. A thin layer of gravel was lightly shovelled over the lid, and, in anticipation of their return to the site, a bright orange tarpaulin was placed over the gravel-covered coffin. Standing around the grave, shovels in hand, they remarked on how garish the fluorescent tarp looked in contrast to the grey surroundings of the quiet grave. 'There will be no trouble in locating the coffin next year with that protecting it,' Kowal said.

With the reconstruction of the surface features of Hartnell's grave complete, the crew readied to leave the island. The plane would come for them in two days – plenty of time to pack, clean the site, and do some more exploring. It was also a time to be alone with their own thoughts. Kowal and Ruszala left for a 35-kilometre hike to Cape Riley and back, while Damkjar and Carlson headed up onto the headland of the island.

Beattie spent the time alone, his mind closed to his surroundings. He brooded about an earlier visit to Beechey Island, a visit made by the explorer Roald Amundsen in August 1903. Amundsen, on his attempt to sail the Northwest Passage, had stopped at Beechey Island to pay tribute to Franklin. It was there, with his small vessel *Gjoa* anchored in Erebus Bay, that Amundsen grappled with the decision of what route to take. Amundsen made the correct one, becoming the first man successfully to sail the elusive passage. As Beattie reflected back on his summer's experience, he did so with a growing feeling that the very freshness of the Franklin sailors' bodies guaranteed the success of his own expedition. Little doubt remained that important new insights into the fate of Franklin and his crews would surface during the months of laboratory work ahead.

The team's final day on Beechey Island, 26 August, was warm and sunny. The tents came down quickly and the gear was carried down by the graves. The gravel in the camping area was smoothed over, and some final bits of paper picked up. Beattie radioed the Polar Shelf base manager in Resolute Bay, and the plane departed to pick them up. Some final photographs were taken of the site, and they set up a tripod to take a group picture. As they were doing this they could just make out the sound of an airplane to the west. In the Arctic there is a sixth sense about airplanes: people will suddenly look up and say 'There's a plane', and everyone will stop what they are doing and listen intently. Usually nothing is heard, but no one doubts that an aircraft is coming. Within a few brief seconds the unmistakable sound of the engine is heard by all.

Soon a Twin Otter hissed by overhead. Everyone waved, the cameras came out, and all watched as the plane made one pass, then circled and landed.

Sitting on the left side of the plane, Beattie looked out at the graves just 10 metres away. During the previous two weeks he had taken hundreds of photographs of all three and had looked into two of them, and yet he felt strangely compelled to take one more photograph through the fogged and scratched window and spinning propeller of the Twin Otter. After pressing the shutter, and before he could wind the camera for a second picture, the plane began to roll. With a roar and two jarring bumps the plane was up and away. Seconds later they were out over Union Bay, turning towards Cornwallis Island visible to the west. Within forty-five minutes they were all sitting in the eating area of the Polar Shelf facilities in Resolute Bay sipping coffee and eating a splendid home-cooked meal the staff had put aside for them. The security and hospitality of the Polar Shelf in Resolute was a marked contrast to the small camp site that had been their home. Already the emotions attached to Beechey Island were fading. Priorities now turned to showers, laundry, and talk. The Pacific Western Airlines jet from the south would arrive the next day, and that meant going home. The season had been a success, but still more exciting discoveries awaited them in their laboratories in Edmonton.

Chapter Ten

THE EVIDENCE MOUNTS

Essentially the body of John Torrington was that of a mummy. What made it so different from mummies recovered from other archaeological sites in the world was the amazing quality of preservation.

When archaeologist Howard Carter opened the three coffins of the Egyptian pharaoh Tutankhamen in the Valley of the Kings, he found the monarch's body in a very bad state of preservation. Dr Douglas Derry, the anatomist who examined Tutankhamen's mummy, wrote a detailed report describing the charred and discoloured remains. The report outlined the damage done through the embalming process and through time: 'the skin of the face is of a greyish colour and is very cracked and brittle . . . the limbs appeared very shrunken and attenuated'.

Even mummies better preserved than Tutankhamen, whether embalmed as a preparation for burial or intentionally desiccated by exposure to sun or air, still suffered major alteration to the appearance, colour and detail of the soft tissues.

The nature of burial can, on rare occasions, result in the unintentional whole or partial preservation of an individual. Some of the best preserved human remains from antiquity have been found in peat bogs in several locations in north-western Europe. In some cases the acids of peat bogs have kept human bodies largely intact not for hundreds but for thousands of years. But those same acids badly discoloured the 'bog people', as they were known, leaving skin 'as if poured in tar' and hair bright red, and helping to decalcify the bones. Another natural means of preservation can result from cold temperatures and lack of moisture. In 1972, 500-year-old mummified human remains, including that of a child, were discovered at Qilakitsoq, Greenland. All of these mummies, however, were rigid and inflexible: the drying and hardening of the tissues having locked the body for ever into the position in which it was buried.

Undoubtedly the most amazing aspect of the Beechey Island research was the discovery of the near-perfect preservation of soft tissue. In effect, the unbroken period of freezing from early 1846 suspended the major outward appearances of decay, allowing John Torrington to look very much as he had in life, right down to the flexibility of the tissue. Even when samples of Torrington's tissues were studied by microscope, some of them looked recent in origin. Other clues, though, reflected the lengthy period of freezing. Details of internal cellular structure were commonly missing, and in most tissues the cells were also partly collapsed. Preservation seemed to vary within the individual. For example, microscope slides made from bowel samples collected from Torrington appeared as if they were taken right out of a text book on modern human histology or pathology, while slides made from other organs showed considerable post-mortem change and loss of detail.

Labaratory results of the autopsy on John Torrington painted a picture of a young man wracked with serious medical problems. Unfortunately, despite careful study of the organ samples by Roger Amy at the University Hospital in Edmonton, a specific cause of death could not be established.

What was most obvious at the time of the autopsy were the blackened lungs, a condition called anthracosis caused by the inhalation of atmospheric pollutants such as tobacco and coal smoke and dust. Also, his lungs were bound to the chest wall by adhesions, a sign of previous lung disease. Microscopically visible destruction of lung tissue identified emphysema, a lung disease normally associated with much older individuals, and evidence of tuberculosis was also seen. Amy's interpretation of the adhesions, and of the presence of fluid in the lung associated with pneumonic infection, suggested to him that pneumonia was probably the ultimate cause of death.

However, it was in the trace element analysis of bone and hair from Torrington that the probable underlying cause of death was found. Atomic absorption analysis of Torrington's bone indicated an elevated amount of lead of 110-151 parts per million (the modern average ranges from 5 to 14 parts per million). Although not as high as those found in the Franklin crewman from Booth Point, the level of bone lead was still many times higher than normal. Torrington would have suffered severe mental and physical problems caused by lead poisoning and, so weakened, finally succumbed to pneumonia.

One theory as to why the Booth Point skeleton had greater lead contamination is that the Franklin sailor found in 1981 lived for over two years longer than John Torrington, thus was exposed to lead on the expedition for a longer period.

Most vital to Beattie's investigation were the results of a trace level analysis conducted on hair. Ten-centimetre-long strands of hair from the nape of Torrington's neck were submitted for laboratory analysis. The hair analysis could tell him if Torrington had been exposed to large amounts of lead. The hair was long enough to show levels of lead ingestion throughout the first eight months of the Franklin expedition. Beattie was astounded by the results of the carefully controlled test. Lead levels in the hair exceeded 600 parts per million, levels indicating acute lead poisoning. Only over the last few centimetres did the level of exposure drop, and then only slightly. This would have been due to a drop in the consumption of food during the last four to eight weeks of Torrington's life, when he was seriously ill.

By combining information gathered from the manner of Torrington's burial, the new information about his physical condition and illnesses, and period accounts of similar burial services conducted in the Arctic, it is possible to recreate his final days, death and burial with some accuracy.

There is no question that during the last couple of weeks of life, John Torrington would have known his time had almost come. Beattie's studies revealed that the petty officer's health had never been good, but in late December 1845, it was different. John Torrington was dying.

He had boarded the *Terror* eight months earlier, doubtless

filled with high hopes. He must have been outwardly healthy when the expedition made its last contact with whaling vessels in late July and early August, or he would have been sent home. Indeed sickness seems to have struck in September, about the same time Franklin's two ships anchored for the winter a few hundred metres off the north-east section of Beechey Island.

It was a slow-moving and lingering illness. The early symptoms of the deadly combination of emphysema and tuberculosis with lead poisoning would have included loss of appetite, irritability, lack of concentration, shortness of breath, and fatigue. Torrington probably continued to work until mid to late November when he would have been sent to the sick bay. The lack of any bed sores on his body shows that during much of December, on the advice of the ship's physician, Torrington would have taken slow walks below decks several times a day. There he could talk with friends, and from time to time, before the illness became severe, look out through the gloom of the arctic winter at the barren, snowswept rock of Beechey Island.

Torrington's physical condition would have worsened dramatically over Christmas. His behaviour would have grown unpredictable, wtih dramatic mood swings that must have caused grave concern to surgeons Alexander Macdonald and John Peddie.

There is no way that these men, with the knowledge and equipment of their time, could have begun to discover the real nature of the illness. All they would have been able to do for Torrington through most of the course of his disease was keep him well-fed and comfortable. Yet despite their attention his weight would have continued slowly dropping to the point of malnutrition. Then, probably during the last days of 1845, he developed pneumonia, a serious blow considering his already diminished state of health. Torrington would never again look out into the arctic night.

Sometime in the days immediately preceding death, Torrington would have given his few possessions to someone who would promise to return them to his father and stepmother when the expedition had sailed through the

Northwest Passage into the Bering Strait and then returned triumphantly to England. Towards the end, the twenty-year-old sailor would have fallen into a delerium, then suffered a series of convulsions before dying on New Year's Day.

News of the expedition's first loss must have spread quickly through the crew of the *Terror*, and the surgeon would have notified Captain Francis Crozier. Within minutes the men of the *Erebus*, including Franklin, would have been informed of John Torrington's death. The surgeons probably debated the cause, going over the protracted and progressive nature of his disease before concluding it was pneumonia complicated by a history of tuberculosis. There was no call for an autopsy.

Torrington's body was carefully cleaned and groomed below decks where the temperature would probably have hovered continually around 10°C. It was 1 January, and his death surely cast a shadow on any New Year celebrations.

After Torrington's body was washed, he was dressed in his shirt and trousers. The two surgeons took care in binding his limbs to his body: one of them wrapped a cotton strip round the body and arms at the level of the elbow, tying a bow at the front; the other quickly tied cotton strips round the big toes, ankles, and thighs.

Above decks, where the ship had been draped with a canvas cover to keep out the snow and some of the cold (the temperature would still be around -10°C), the carpenter, Thomas Honey, and his mate Alexander Wilson began carefully constructing the coffin, Macdonald having provided them with Torrington's measurements. They used a stock timber, mahogany, measuring ¾ inch (1.9 cm) thick by 12 inches (30.5 cm) wide. The lid and coffin bottom were each constructed of three pieces: a long central piece with shaped sections attached by dowels to each side. The box was constructed of the same type of wood, and the curves at the shoulder were produced by kerfing (making a series of parallel cuts across the inside width of the board, allowing it to be bent without breaking). Square iron nails were used to secure all the sections together.

The coffin lid and box were carefully wrapped in navy blue wool material which was held in place by narrow, white cotton ribbons nailed to the coffin and outlining its contours. Torrington's messmates had taken great care in preparing the labelled metal plaque which was to be attached to the outside of the coffin lid. Another task of the carpenters, under the direction of one of *Terror*'s lieutenants, was the preparation of an inscribed headboard.

Carrying picks and shovels, a small group of seamen from the *Terror* then walked the few hundred metres from the ship to a location on the island just upslope from the armourer's forge.

They used their feet and shovels to sweep away a thin layer of snow from a small area of beach gravel. In the bitter cold, where the earth seemed like iron, they must have wondered about the seemingly backbreaking work they'd been assigned. But Franklin had ordered a proper burial, as close as circumstances would permit to that which John Torrington would have received in his native Manchester. After perhaps a few brief words, several of the seamen grabbed a pickaxe each.

The digging would have been treacherous and difficult, illuminated only by lamp light. In the near darkness the pickaxes would have sent up showers of sparks as they struck against the icy earth. As the sailors took turns to hack at the ground in the deepening grave, they finally reached a depth of 1.45 metres.

Preparations for the burial of John Torrington would have taken a day or two, but finally the small, slender coffin was lowered on ropes over the ship's side down to the ice a few metres below. It was probably then secured to a small sledge and no doubt draped with a flag.

A party of seamen picked up the ropes secured to the front of the sledge and began to drag it slowly over the ice and snow towards the grave site. If Beattie's own experience of King William Island was any indication, it must have been a tortuous trail, with small hummocks of ice preventing them from dragging the coffin in a straight line. Instead, they would have had to zigzag towards the shore.

A small procession would have followed, probably made up of Torrington's messmates and friends from the *Terror*, and led by Sir John Franklin, Captain Francis Crozier, Commander James Fitzjames, and some of the *Terror*'s officers.

Someone carried the wooden headboard, a monument not only to Torrington but in the event to the whole expedition.

A layer of snow found on the coffin lid by Beattie and his team shows that a light snow was falling that day early in January 1846. The men who stayed on the ships probably watched as, man by man, the procession was swallowed by the snow. Soon all that could have been seen were the lamps, flickering and swaying like fireflies around the shadows of the invisible party. Then they too disappeared.

Franklin probably presided at the burial. He was a deeply religious man who, eight months earlier, had asked the British Admiralty to furnish one hundred Bibles, prayer books and testaments for sale at cost aboard the ships.

The snow, a spiralling yellow curtain in the lamp light, swirled around the group standing at the graveside. Some sifted and settled into the grave, obscuring the last view of Torrington's coffin. Each breath of Franklin's would have been made visible by the gripping cold, the sound of his voice blending with the icy, penetrating wind that always seems to blow at Beechey Island.

His words were probably brief, but presented with an obvious reverence and sincerity. Quickly, the ceremony was over, and thoughts turned away from the young man who just months before at Woolwich, near London, had joined Franklin's carefully selected crew a relatively healthy man.

In many ways Torrington's was an uneventful death, yet the confirmation of high lead levels in his body was of great significance in the context of the entire expedition. Beattie had stepped beyond the conventional theories about the expedition's end.

It seemed clear that the startling proof of lead poisoning in Torrington, coupled with the results from the Booth Point skeleton, demonstrated that lead had played an important if not pivotal role in the Franklin disaster. Lost was the romanticized and safe version of scurvy and starvation alone carrying off the expedition. The medical findings from Torrington opened the door on a whole new way of looking at this and other nineteenth-century expeditions. But such a radical new theory about the underlying cause of the destruction of one of history's great voyages of discovery needed to be backed up by as much evidence as possible. The more bodies demonstrating lead contamination, the more credible it was that the theory applied to the whole expedition.

The discoveries made during 1984 only served to underline the importance of returning to Beechey Island and establishing the cause of death of Hartnell and Braine. Besides, an important part of the investigation was also to establish what conditions must have been like on the expedition during 1845-6, and to reconstruct the last months and days in the lives of the three men buried at Beechey Island. Their bodies provided an unprecedented and privileged opportunity to look into British and Canadian history – a three-dimensional history, represented by the only true 'survivors' of Franklin's expedition.

After the 1984 field season ended and news of the preservation of John Torrington and John Hartnell was announced, two indirect descendants of Hartnell contacted Beattie. Donald Bray of Croydon, England, was astonished to see coverage of Beattie's expedition and to hear the name of his ancestor mentioned. Bray, a retired sub-postmaster, had devoted years to tracing his family history and was in possession of rare letters and documents which added haunting insights into Hartnell's family and life.

Most touching were two letters to John and Thomas Hartnell, one sent by their mother Sarah and the other by their brother Charles, which were intended to greet the sailors upon their completion of the Northwest Passage. The two men never received the letters, dated 23 December 1847. John Hartnell had already been dead for nearly two years and Thomas's death probably came the following summer on King William Island.

'My Dear Children,' Sarah Hartnell's letter began, 'It is a great pleasure to me to have a chance to write you. I hope you are both well. I assure you I have many anxious moments about you but I endeavour to cast my prayers on Him who is too good to be unkind'. After a reference to her own illness and other news about family and friends, the letter ended: 'If it is the Lord's will may we be spared to meet on earth. If not God

128

grant we may all meet around His throne to praise Him to all eternity'. Perhaps Sarah knew, as parents sometimes do, that her sons were facing their deaths.

Another descendant of John Hartnell would, along with three other specialists, join Beattie's scientific team when he returned to the field in 1986. Brian Spenceley, a professor at Lakehead University in Thunder Bay, Ontario, and a great-great-nephew of Hartnell, would soon be able to experience that which no other man has, to look into the eyes of a relative who has been dead for more than a century.

Chapter Eleven

ICEMAN REVISITED

Jumping out of the Twin Otter onto the snow-blanketed ground of Beechey Island, Beattie was temporarily blinded by the bright, sunny sky and the sun's rays reflecting off the white ground. Only gradually did major geographical features and the three tiny headstones that poked their way through the snow become visible, assuring him that he was again on the island where so many memories lay.

This time Beattie planned to complete his examinations of the Franklin graveyard. Part of the research team arrived with Beattie from Resolute on 8 June 1986. That group, consisting of archaeologist Eric Damkjar, project photographer Brian Spenceley, historical consultant Dr Jim Savelle (who was a co-investigator with Beattie during the 1981 season and now served as a research scholar at the Scott Polar Research Institute) and field assistants Arne Carlson, Walt Kowal and Joelee Nungaq would set up camp and then conduct the detailed archaeological work and exhumations. A team of specialists consisting of pathologist Dr Roger Amy, radiologist Dr Derek Notman, radiology technician Larry Anderson and arctic clothing specialist Barbara Schweger would arrive one week later.

Beattie started his 1986 field season earlier than that of 1984 in order to avoid the problem of water run-off from melting snow. But as the temperatures remained below freezing in June, and a brisk wind swept across the island for a good number of days, heightening the cold, the investigators had to endure additional hardships.

Each of the crew quickly set to work to establish camp,

consisting of the usual array of individual and communal tents, with one new addition being a 5-metre-tall flag pole where the bright red and white Canadian flag snapped in the near constant winds, along with the flag of the Northwest Territories. During this work, however, Beattie's mind was fixed on something else. For two years one question had nagged him. It was a question posed by almost everyone he had talked to about the research on Beechey Island: was there any guarantee the bodies of John Torrington and John Hartnell were again encased in ice after their 1984 reburials? The theory that the summer meltwater would trickle down into the filled-in excavation, seep into the coffin, and subsequently freeze was a good, logical one. But Beattie wondered if the process were so simple. The 1984 exhumation of John Torrington was final and complete; there could be no verification of the theory there. However, uncovering John Hartnell, exposed once in 1852 and again in 1984, would soon answer the question.

A tent was again erected over the grave to protect the exhumation process from the elements. As before, digging was extremely difficult. The exposure of Hartnell's coffin required twenty-four hours of continual digging by Kowal, Carlson, Savelle and Nungaq. The process had now become almost mechanical. One person would labour with the pickaxe until either the pain in his hands or the exhaustion in his arms required rest. The loosened ice and gravel would then be shovelled into buckets by one or two of the excavators, lifted out of the grave to another of them, and finally dumped on the growing pile of 'back-dirt'. Conversation between the excavators began with recollections of previous archaeological digs, especially those of 1984, but as the hours passed, the relentless sound of the pickaxe, broken regularly by the rasping, fingernail-on-blackboard sound of the shovel pushing into resistant gravel and ice, eventually won out.

When the coffin lid was finally exposed, and the limits of the coffin identified, the group took a long overdue rest and waited for the arrival of the team of specialists. To this point the excavation was a replay of 1984. But the next step, the removal of the coffin lid, though also done in 1984, would this time provide an answer to the question of the refreezing of the bodies. They were therefore poised on the true beginnings of the 1986 investigations.

During the break in the exhumation work, Beattie and Damkjar returned to the food tin dump for a more detailed survey than the one they had conducted in 1984. Two days were spent thoroughly documenting what was left of the tins. Out of the original 700 or so, fragments of fewer than 150 remained. Tins are a very transportable, recognizable, and desired artefact for amateur archaeologists and collectors. Over the decades people had been depleting the information pool represented by the containers. None of those remaining was complete, and most were badly fragmented. But all portions of the tins were represented, including the soldered seams.

The area of the tin scatter was gridded with string and tied in to a datum point. Each square metre of the grid was photographed and searched, and every tin fragment located and described. All of the larger pieces and those with particularly good features were individually photographed. Samples of 'ordinary' tins were collected for later study, as well as some tins with especially good examples of the poor soldering and manufacture.

On the second day of work at the can dump, Beattie and Damkjar were interrupted by Nungaq, who had been out hiking on the ice of Union Bay during the break in the digging. He came walking quickly along the spit towards them, his dog Keena held tightly by her chain. 'There's a bear coming,' he said as he trotted up the rise of the mound. Pointing west he continued: 'Look, over there, it's coming right for us'. Little interest in the tins remained as Beattie and Damkjar squinted out over the bright field of ice. Then Beattie saw it. Its head was lowered and it did not appear to be moving at all, though its body was swaying slightly from side to side. From this quick glimpse he recalled an important lesson. He remembered when he was a student pilot and his instructor lectured him: 'If you spot another airplane coming your way and it appears to be moving, you're safe – just keep your eye on it. But if that plane looks like it is standing still, watch out, because it's coming straight for you.' A strange thing to recall at this particular time, but the rule still applied. Though the bear was a good distance away, perhaps a kilometre, it looked awfully big. Within minutes they were all heading back to camp, cameras swinging from their necks, clutching notebooks, tripods, and rifles. They did not want to leave either expensive camera equipment or their collected data at the tin dump for the bear to play with, so they had filled their arms with everything they had taken to the site. Halfway back to camp, they turned to see the bear crossing the spit in a slow, purposeful gait. They breathed easier when they watched the bear stop for a moment to test the air, and then move on, heading across Erebus Bay to Devon Island.

The Twin Otter carrying Amy, Notman, Anderson and Schweger at last swept over the camp. Beattie noticed right away that skis had been strapped onto the tundra wheels of the aircraft. The thin layer of snow on the island made a landing there impossible; the plane would have to land offshore, on ice-covered Erebus Bay. That meant that the heavy load of equipment on board, over half the 1,500 kilograms of equipment used during the research, would have to be carried across the ice and up the beach to their camp. After brief greetings, the eleven-member team watched the Twin Otter leave, then spent the next two hours at the difficult task.

Exhumation work resumed with the digging of a work area adjacent to the right side of the coffin. This exposed the coffin's side for the first time, and immediately something of interest was discovered: three 'handles' were found spaced along the side of the coffin wall. However, these were not real handles like the ones on Torrington's coffin, but symbolic representations made out of the same white linen tape that decorated the edges of the coffin.

As in 1984, the team used heated water to accelerate the thawing process. As there was no running water on the island, Kowal developed a highly efficient method of melting snow, providing a constant though meagre water source for the melting process. The water was heated, two buckets at a time, on naphtha stoves located in the adjacent autopsy/x-ray tent. When ready, Kowal carried the buckets across to Carlson and Nungaq who would slowly pour the water over the dark blue covered coffin. When too much water had accumulated in the bottom of the grave, making work virtually impossible, an electric sump pump was lowered in. The water drawn out of the grave was directed through a hose away from the excavation area. It seemed to Beattie that the thawing was much more difficult than it had been in 1984, and the time of year probably accounted for the difference. Though they did not test the temperature of the permafrost in 1984 or 1986, it seemed that at every depth it was colder in June than in August.

After photographs of the cleaned coffin were taken, and it was measured (203.5 cm by 48 cm by 33 cm deep), the delicate task of loosening and removing the already damaged lid was started. When at last it was lifted, Beattie and Carlson could see immediately that Hartnell's right arm area and face, both exposed in 1984, were again completely encased in ice. 'Well, the water flowed back in, didn't it?' Beattie said. The question had been answered. Standing by Hartnell's ice-protected body, Beattie thought about the condition of John Torrington only a few steps away. He was now satisfied that the young petty officer was again suspended in time by the very processes that had allowed them a brief, privileged glimpse in 1984.

Damkjar, standing alongside the upper edge of the grave with the others, pointed out that the ice around Hartnell appeared quite discoloured. The ice in the centre of the block, about where Hartnell's chest should be, was not an opaque white as with Torrington, but very brownish, even mottled.

Soon the work of exposing the body began, the warm water quickly unveiling the features of the seaman's face. This was an overwhelming experience for Spenceley, Hartnell's great-great-nephew, who stood close by the grave's edge, gazing in silence at his own family history over a distance of 140 years.

There did not seem to be any major deterioration in the tissues during the two-year hiatus. One observation made in 1984 was that Hartnell's left eye was well preserved while his right eye appeared to be damaged, either while he lived or somehow shortly after his death. Inglefield's reports on the exhumation he and Sutherland had conducted in 1852 had not indicated any problem with Hartnell's right eye. In 1986 Beattie noticed immediately that, in addition to the shrunken right eye, Hartnell's left eye showed some shrinkage as well. It is likely that exposure, for even a brief period, caused changes peculiar to the eyes, leaving the rest of the external features unaffected. In other words, the exposure of Hartnell in 1852 probably induced changes in the right eye – the fact that the left eye appeared normal to the researchers in 1984 indicates that Inglefield and Sutherland probably did not expose the left side of the face. The shrinking of the left eye over the two years that had passed since its exposure in 1984 supported the theory.

As the ice surrounding Hartnell thawed, it became apparent that he was wrapped in a white shroud from his shoulders down. The damaged shirtsleeve on his right arm was exposed through a tear in the sheet and pieces of the coffin lid appeared to have been driven forcibly into his right chest wall during the 1852 exhumation. When the obscuring ice was melted higher up the arm, the tears in the shroud, shirtsleeve, and now-visible undergarments were continued as scissor or knife cuts. Obviously, to fully expose Hartnell's arm, Sutherland had had to make cuts in the shroud and clothing. This evidence showed that the investigation of Hartnell's body in 1852 was limited to his face and right arm. It would have been too difficult and taken too much time for Sutherland to do more.

On Hartnell's head was a toque-like hat, which in turn was resting on a small frilled pillow stuffed with wood shavings. Thawing of the ice surrounding the body continued until Hartnell was completely exposed. Nothing was moved by the group until the shrouded body had been thoroughly described and photographed. The next stage was the folding back of the shroud, which took a very long time because only the very thinnest layer of the exposed shroud and body was actually thawed and additional thawing of the fabric was required.

As Hartnell was unwrapped from the shroud his left arm was exposed, followed by his right arm. Immediately, Amy and Beattie could see that the arms had been bound to the body in the same manner as was seen on Torrington, though this time the material used was light brown wool. However, his right hand was lying on an outside fold of the binding. It was clear that his right arm had been extracted by Sutherland and, when his examination was complete, he had not tucked the hand back underneath the binding but left it lying on top.

Hartnell's blue and white striped shirt was of a similar pattern to that seen on Torrington, though the stripes were not printed but woven (a more expensive material than that found on Torrington) and the design was also different from Torrington's. It was a pull-over style, and some of the front buttons were missing, the buttonholes being tied shut with loops of string. The lower portion of the shirt had two letters embroidered on it in red and the date '1844'. The letters appeared to be 'TH', and it may be that the shirt had originally belonged to John Hartnell's elder brother and expedition companion, Thomas.

Underneath the shirt was a wool sweater-like undergarment, and beneath that a cotton undershirt. He was not wearing trousers, stockings, or footwear.

Beattie and Schweger were puzzled that Hartnell should have had three layers of clothing covering his upper body and nothing on below the waist. They suspect that there may have been a viewing of the body aboard the *Erebus* prior to burial, with the man's lower half covered by the shroud.

Hartnell's legs and feet were slightly darkened and very shrunken and emaciated by illness, and in part by the freezing. Like Torrington, his toes were tied together. In preparation for the temporary removal of Hartnell's body for the x-ray examination and autopsy, the shroud was completely pulled back, and his cap removed, revealing a full head of very dark brown, nearly black, hair, parted on his left. Without his hat he lost much of the sinister look which first confronted the scientists in the summer of 1984. Instead, he appeared to be simply a young man who, for some mysterious reason, had died at the age of twenty-five on 4 January 1846.

Now began the most difficult and unpleasant phase of the exposure. Even as Hartnell lay in the coffin, apparently ready to be gently lifted out, his body was still part of the permafrost, solidly frozen to the mass of ice below. Slowly and carefully, water had to be directed underneath the body, freeing it millimetres at a time. The permafrost had a grip that would not let go without a fight. Finally the scientists won the battle, and the body was freed.

Before lifting Hartnell from his coffin, his right thumbnail was removed, and samples of hair from his scalp, beard and pubic area were collected for later examination and analysis.

Beattie, Carlson, and Nungaq then lifted the body out of the grave onto a white linen sheet where it was immediately wrapped. Hartnell was carried a distance of three metres to the autopsy/x-ray tent where Notman and Anderson prepared to take a series of x-rays of him while he was clothed. Still frozen to the bottom of the coffin were Hartnell's nineteenth-century shroud, and beneath that a folded woollen blanket. Damkjar, over the next day, struggled to remove these two items. When they were finally freed, they were handed over to Schweger for analysis and sampling.

Notman and Anderson had already set up their x-ray 'clinic' inside the autopsy tent. The next order of business was the assembly of the darkroom tent. Beattie had provided them with the inside dimensions of the long-house tent months before, and using these they had designed a unique, collapsible, and portable darkroom. The structure consisted of a tubular metal frame which was screwed together and over which a double layer of thick black plastic (cut, formed, and taped together) was pulled and tucked in along the floor. On one side they had fashioned a door from a double overlap of the plastic cover, forming a light trap. Inside the darkroom Anderson had just enough room to stand and manoeuvre around the chemical tubs. A mechanical timer was hung inside as well as a battery-operated safe light.

Kowal gave them a hand in melting the 500 litres of clean, strained water required for the x-ray film development. Four large Coleman stoves were running in the tent constantly, and Kowal would bring in buckets of snow to melt. When a bucket was ready it was poured through a fine strainer directly into the large plastic garbage bins they had brought as chemical holders. When the tubs were finally filled with water (which took a whole day), Anderson mixed his chemicals. He made wood-framed structures to hold the film sheets in their development frames, and these were lowered into the tubs. A 200-watt aquarium heater was then immersed in the liquid, which would bring the temperature up to the 20° thought necessary to provide controlled development.

The x-ray unit was a remarkably compact yet powerful instrument mounted on four tubular steel legs. Too fragile to risk being sent from their clinic at the Park Nicollet Medical Centre in Minneapolis as normal freight, Notman and Anderson had bought an airplane ticket for it, and everyone had a good laugh when they told how the machine, named Fragile Bulky Notman on its ticket, had 'sat' in the first-class section at the front of the Northwest Orient plane during the flight into Canada while they had to sit back in the economy class.

When in use, the machine would be lifted over the body, and the legs positioned firmly in the gravel. A focusing light beam on the bottom of the unit would then be turned on to illuminate and define the area to be x-rayed before a film plate was slid under the body.

Notman and Anderson tested their x-ray set-up on a polar bear scapula, found lying on one of the beach ridges near the grave site. The results were very encouraging: holding the x-ray up, Notman described the bony details of the scapula to the others. Though they had been told by a number of experts that they were not likely to succeed in getting satisfactory x-rays under such difficult field conditions, his voice betrayed a note of gleeful triumph and self-satisfaction. Anderson's face also seemed to say, 'Well, they were all wrong! I knew we could do it!'

With this air of success, Notman and Anderson began the difficult job of x-raying the clothed John Hartnell. The x-ray area on the ground adjacent to the door was the same as where the autopsy was to be performed. When an exposure was to be made, either Notman or Anderson would put on a heavy, full-length lead apron, and all other people in the tent would line up behind them. A loud call of 'exposing' would be made for the benefit of people working outside the tent so that they could move away to a safe distance of at least 30 metres before the exposure was made.

Anderson would then take the film plate into the darkroom for processing. Ten to fifteen minutes later he would emerge with the dripping film, which he hung by pegs to clotheslines stretched across the length of the tent. He and Notman would then examine the quality of the film and decide if there was any need to change their technique.

When the initial x-raying of Hartnell had been completed, Notman, Anderson, and Amy stood in front of the row of hanging film to begin the preliminary examination. Anderson quickly pointed to the first x-ray: 'He's got a solid block of ice in his head'. The frozen brain tissue obscured the x-ray image, meaning they'd have to x-ray again after further thawing. Looking at the chest x-rays, Notman pointed at a small feature near Hartnell's neck. 'We've got our first metallic object,' he said. 'It looks like a ring on its side'. In fact, the metal was the frame of a decorative, embroidered button. The chest x-rays were confusing in that the internal organs appeared uncharacteristic and of unusual and varied densities – an unexpected series of observations on the first x-rays ever to be taken under such circumstances. In fact, except for the details of the bones, little could be determined, let alone identified from these first x-rays. Beattie wondered if the preservation, which appeared so good to the eye, was in fact not good enough to allow x-ray information to be collected. Notman was frustrated with these first findings for, even in the desiccated and eviscerated Egyptian mummies he had studied in the past there had always been some recognizable details in his x-rays. Only the autopsy would provide the answers.

It had been difficult to position the body with the clothing still on, and, spurred on by the confusing results of the first x-rays, Notman and Anderson wanted to try again after the clothing had been removed. Beattie, Amy, Nungaq and Schweger began the difficult task of unclothing Hartnell. 'What we'll do is ask the patient to sit up,' Amy said, a request for Beattie and Schweger to support the body while he attempted to remove the outer shirt. Trained in the medical field, Amy, Notman, and Anderson always referred to the sailors as patients, reflecting their strictly professional attitude towards medical procedures and research, even in these extraordinary circumstances. After some initial attempts to slip the clothes over Hartnell's head and off his limbs, it was decided that it would be necessary to cut the fabric. To minimize damage to the clothes, Beattie made a single vertical cut up the back of each garment. Doing this avoided the over-extension of the limbs, as well as preventing stress being placed on the material, which could have caused tearing both in the fabric and along the seams. As the clothes slipped off the body the scientists made a truly astonishing discovery.

'Son of a bitch, he's already been autopsied! Son of a gun!' said Amy. 'We've got an upside down "Y" incision. This sort or thing has not been seen before, this is absolutely unique'.

Running down John Hartnell's chest and abdomen was a sutured incision that left no doubt that in the short hours after his death a surgeon on the *Erebus*, probably assistant-surgeon Dr Harry D.S. Goodsir, who was an anatomist by training, had attempted to establish the cause of death. It's no wonder Amy was so excited at this discovery. Here he had an unprecedented opportunity to view the handiwork of a medical predecessor of long ago. And by conducting his own autopsy, Amy would actually be assisting this long-dead doctor. The surgeon of the *Erebus* certainly anticipated that he would bring the information from his autopsy back to England. Now the information would finally be known.

This important discovery begged the question: why had the surgeon conducted an autopsy? To find out the cause of death, obviously; but what had prompted the decision? Perhaps the death of John Torrington of the *Terror* only three days before was part of the reason. There may also have been some symptoms associated with Hartnell's death that left serious doubt in the minds of the surgeons as to the cause of death. A challenge faced Amy who had to sort through the riddle.

The standard incision in an autopsy performed today is 'Y'-shaped, with the arms of the 'Y' extending down from each shoulder and meeting at the base of the sternum (breastbone). From this point the incision continues down to the pubic bone. In the case of Hartnell's autopsy, the incision was upside down: the arm of the 'Y' originated near the point of each hip, meeting near the umbilicus (belly button) and extending up to the top of the sternum. The procedures for autopsy technique in the mid-nineteenth century are not well represented in scientific literature. Beattie wondered if the incision indicated that the surgeon was concentrating on the bowel, or whether this was the habitual procedure for autopsy followed by the surgeon. Amy was later able to reconstruct, step by step, what the original pathologist had done. The extent and direction taken during this first autopsy provided clues to the suspicions held by the surgeon relating to the cause of death.

Dr Harry D. S. Goodsir

That an autopsy had been done solved the mystery of the strange x-rays: the surgeon of the *Erebus* had removed the organs for examination, and then replaced them in one mixed mass. Not surprisingly, this resulted in a meaningless collection of soft tissue detail in the first x-rays taken by Notman and Anderson. Also, the brownish discoloration seen in the ice when the lid was first removed probably resulted from blood and other fluids seeping out of the incision when water filled the coffin during the summer of 1846.

After Notman and Anderson had completed a second series of x-rays, a process that took another six hours, making a total of fourteen hours of x-raying, they retired for a well-deserved rest, but not before a slightly hair-raising experience. The x-raying continued into the late hours of the day, and most of the crew had retired to their tents. Savelle and Nungaq were sitting in the kitchen tent talking. Beattie was in the autopsy/x-ray tent, more as company for Notman and Anderson than as help. Keena, the dog brought along to serve as a watch for polar bears, was tethered outside the kitchen tent and could be heard whining in her familiar, annoying way. Suddenly Keena stopped whining – unusual in itself. But then she barked madly. The three men in the autopsy/x-ray tent looked at each other. They had never heard her bark before, and they knew that there had to be a good reason: a bear. Then they heard the 'pop pop pop' of rifles being fired and off in the distance voices shouting, 'Bear, bear in camp!' Beattie reached for the rifle he had brought down to the tent and slowly stuck his head out. The tents over the graves and the autopsy/x-ray tent were separated from the main grouping by about 100 metres and, peering round the edge of Braine's tent back towards the main camp, he saw a bear standing in the open space. Notman and Anderson were now beside Beattie, sizing up the situation. Beattie had Kowal's gun, one with which he was not familiar – and sure enough the bolt jammed twice, but the third and final bullet went into the chamber cleanly. Notman, in looking around for some other weapon, grabbed a shovel. Anderson had his camera. So armed, the three stayed behind Braine's tent out of sight of the bear which soon became annoyed at the noise of guns and people. It began to amble off, angling towards the beach. Passing downwind of the graves, just 20 metres away, it caught the scent of the three, and of John Hartnell. As it paused with its nose in the air, Beattie thought, 'Oh, brother, it's gonna come this way'. But then he heard 'twang twang twang' as three bullets ricocheted off the gravel beside the bear, forcing it back into a slow retreat, and the crisis ended as it ambled down the beach and out onto the ice. From that point on during the summer, someone always stayed outside keeping watch with the dog. From the bear tracks in the snow Nungaq was able to determine that it had come in off the ice close to the kitchen tent, chased some gulls, wandered up to the food cache beside the kitchen tent, saw the dog, and decided to sniff it out. No wonder Keena had barked: when people started to pop their heads out of tents to see what the commotion was all about, the bear and the dog were nose to nose. Keena was lucky. Notman, Anderson, and Beattie were lucky. It may have been close to the end of a long day but none of the crew were ready for sleep now.

With the x-raying complete, Amy and Beattie, dressed in green surgical gowns, white aprons and blue surgical caps, began the autopsy. Hartnell was first measured and weighed. He was taller and heavier than Torrington, at 180 centimetres (5 feet 11 inches) and 45 kilograms (7 stone). Amy then reopened the inverted 'Y' incision by cutting the original sutures. He noted that several knife cuts were made on the surface of the chest plate before the ribs had been successfully divided during the original autopsy. It soon became obvious that Franklin's surgeons had not focused their attention on the bowel, as their incision suggested, but apparently believed the cause of Hartnell's death concerned the heart and lungs. In the earlier autopsy, Dr Goodsir had removed the heart with part of the trachea. He would first have held the heart up to look at its apex for signs of disease; then he made two cuts, one each into the right and left ventricles, to look at the valves. When he had finished with the heart, he dissected the roots of the lungs to look for evidence of tuberculosis and made a few cuts into the liver looking for confirmation of the disease. Hartnell's bowel was untouched. On completion of the autopsy, Dr Goodsir replaced Hartnell's chest plate (the anterior portion of the ribs and the sternum) upside down. The original autopsy turned out to have been a cursory one that could have been conducted in less than half an hour. During his investigations the surgeon of the Erebus would have found confirmation of tuberculosis of the lungs. Once observations about the original autopsy had been completed, Amy began his own much more detailed investigation. Beattie labelled the sample containers and sealed the samples handed to him by Amy, while Spenceley photographed the proceedings in great detail.

First, any frozen water from inside the body was collected as these fluids would have come from the tissues. Then, after sterilizing his surgical instruments in the open flame of a naphtha stove, Amy cut a frozen piece from each of the organs and placed them in a sterile container which was promptly sealed and kept frozen in a cooler. These samples would later undergo bacteriological analysis in the laboratory. Other samples of organs and tissue were then taken and placed in preservative, these would later be studied under a microscope. Amy occasionally made observations about the condition of Hartnell, such as describing the state of blood vessels: 'Vessels don't contain blood, they contain ice and the ice is clear.' Many of the organs were found to be in a fair state of preservation, although the brain had turned to liquid. Finally, bone was cut with a surgical saw from the femur, rib, lumbar vertebra and skull. From start to finish, which ended with Amy resuturing the original 1846 incision, the autopsy took the three men nine hours to complete. It had been very thorough.

Everyone was exhausted, yet work was continuing nearby in Braine's tent in preparation for his exposure. Hartnell's body was tightly wrapped in the autopsy sheet and carried into his own tent. When Schweger finished documenting the Hartnell fabrics the group began to arrange for his reburial. The blanket was repositioned in the bottom of the coffin and the original shroud laid back in position. His body was passed down into the grave and then put back in the coffin. The shroud was then closed over him, and it was soon time for their final moment with the young sailor.

Just before midnight on 18 June they all gathered in Hartnell's tent. Schweger had brought the clothing wrapped in mylar, an inert material that would protect and support the clothes. Spenceley and Beattie jumped down into the grave, and Schweger passed them each item of clothing, which they placed carefully alongside the shrouded body. Once this was complete, the lid was lowered down to them, but as they tried positioning it on the coffin they could not get it to fit as they had found it – a layer of ice had formed on the top edge of the coffin, and this had to be chipped away before the lid would fall into its proper place. Beattie took the small chisel hammer and removed the ice within a few minutes, and the reburial continued. Spenceley and Beattie, helped out of the grave by the others, now joined the ring of researchers standing at the graveside. A spontaneous moment of silence was punctuated by the sound of the wind snapping the tent flaps, and the sorrowful howling of Keena. 'One hundred and forty years ago his brother was standing in this same spot,' Beattie said at last, breaking the silence.

Slowly the group filed out of the tent, and with hardly a word spoken, they all began to fill buckets with gravel and complete the process of reburial. At this time none of them could fail to feel the transience of human existence and the reality of death. Exhuming Hartnell had been a hard thing for them to do, something very difficult to deal with. But now it was finished and, for the moment, there was relief that this one door was closing on their project. But in the tent next to them, the excavation of Private William Braine of the Royal Marines had already uncovered a surprise – one of many that awaited them.

Chapter Twelve

THE ROYAL MARINE

As with Torrington's and Hartnell's graves, a string grid was placed over Braine's grave. Damkjar made scale drawings of the surface features in each square metre of the grid, while Spenceley, hovering on a ladder over his tripod-mounted camera, took a series of Polaroid photographs to be used during the reconstruction.

On the snow beside the grave the crew assembled another long-house tent. This was lifted over the headboard and positioned over the grave, allowing some manoeuvring space at each side of the structure. The tent was then tied to Hartnell's tent, and the corners secured to large metal pegs driven into the permafrost.

Excavation began with trowels and buckets. The gravel covering the grave, and filling the spaces between the limestone rocks, was removed by trowelling, and during this cleaning process a few artefacts were found which had, over the decades, worked their way into the cracks and corners of the grave. The exact positions of these objects, mainly wood fragments and bird bones, were recorded in reference to the string grid which still covered the grave. One of the large, slab-like limestone rocks was covered with a mat of gravel consolidated by a well-established colony of mosses, and the crew did not disturb this tiny islet of vegetation. They lifted the huge rock intact so that the eventual reconstruction of the grave would include the micro-garden.

One of the distinctive features of Braine's grave was the highly structured nature of the surface features. The overall impression was that it represented a crypt, and the detail of parts of the

146

structure seemed to confirm this. A major challenge to the excavators would be the accurate reconstruction of the grave. As the rocks were removed identification numbers and orientation indicators were penned on their undersides. They were then carried outside the tent and placed in rows on the snow, the larger rocks being used as anchoring weights for the edge of the tent.

Two hours were spent in identifying and removing nearly one hundred rocks from the surface of the grave. One of the more interesting of the large rocks was the roughly circular slab lying on the surface at the foot of the grave. Two-thirds of the exposed surface had a black coloration which Savelle said had been applied to the grave by Penny in 1853-4. When the rock was upended they saw that the underside was nearly completely painted black. It was apparent that this rock had at one time been standing at the foot of the grave, and had functioned as the footboard seen in some of the engravings and paintings made at the site during the 1850s.

The next step, after all the rocks had been removed, was to begin the now familiar task of removing the permafrost. Kowal, Carlson, Savelle, and Nungaq began digging and, eighteen hours later, they encountered the first signs of Braine's coffin. The excavation of Braine's grave exemplified the determination of the crew, as they worked virtually non-stop for a total of 37 hours until the goal had been reached and the coffin completely exposed. Braine had been buried very deeply, down 2 metres in the permafrost, and his coffin turned out to be the largest of the three – 211 cm by 49 cm by 33 cm deep. This combination resulted in the removal of considerably more permafrost than from either Torrington's or Hartnell's graves: all four sides of Braine's grave excavation had to be extended as the size of the coffin became obvious.

As the final centimetres of permafrost were picked away, the texture softened, signalling the approach of the coffin. Aware that both Torrington and Hartnell had been buried with plaques attached to their coffin lids, Kowal explored carefully the position on the lid where a plaque would have been placed. One of the thrills of archaeology is that discoveries, even those that are predictable because of previous experience, are invariably a surprise. The discovery of Braine's plaque was no exception: the first, small exposure of the plaque had a completely unexpected appearance. It was copper-coloured, and as the exposure was enlarged, Kowal could see that it was metal, with the green–blue of copper oxidation showing on the small portion of the edge that had been carefully exposed. Kowal continued to widen the window over the plaque, which seemed to be extensive. The words punched into the metal began to emerge, and eventually the whole plaque was uncovered. It was huge, 33 cm by 44 cm, and great care had obviously been taken in its preparation. The plaque read: 'w. BRAINE R.M. 8 CO. W.D. H.M.S. EREBUS DIED APRIL 3rd, 1846 AGED 33 YEARS.'

The '4' in 1846 was backwards. Everyone was thrilled by the preservation and quality of the plaque, which, while constructed differently from Torrington's, was just as touching. With a lot of digging still to do, the plaque was covered by a piece of plastic and a thin layer of gravel to protect it during the continuing exposure of the whole coffin.

The coffin lid appeared to be in excellent condition, and Carlson felt that he could remove the lid without shearing the nails, but by carefully prying with a crowbar. He began slowly, but the nails pulled free quickly and within twenty minutes the lid was loose and ready to be lifted off. Carlson and Beattie, one at each end, lifted the lid slowly and gently straight up, supporting it on their arms as they passed it up to Nungaq and Damkjar, who took it straight out of the tent.

'I see some bright red,' Carlson said, as all the researchers peered at an area of blood-red ice covering Braine's face. Beattie glanced along the length of the coffin. He could see part of a shroud over the chest area. In direct contact with the coffin lid, it had not been obscured by the opaque ice which filled the rest of the coffin. When the thawing was started, the red colour over Braine's face quickly took on texture and shape. It was a kerchief of Asian design with a pattern of leaves printed in black and white. As the ice melted in the rest of the coffin, the outline of the whole shroud was soon determined.

Within a few hours the upper half of the enshrouded body had been exposed. It was the most arresting vision the researchers had experienced at the site. The outline and contours of the body could be perceived in the ivory coloured shroud, but the sight was dominated by the bright red kerchief lying over Braine's face. The vivid colour seemed so out of place deep within the grave, and the filmy nature of the material caused it to cling tightly to the face it covered, accentuating the outlines of Braine's brow, his nose, chin, and cheeks; and in the centre, behind small tears in the kerchief, the black oval of his partly opened mouth was visible. Poking through the tears were some incisor teeth, producing a frightening, scarlet grin which left every one of the crew transfixed for a time.

The edges of the kerchief were still frozen deep in the recesses of the coffin bottom, and it was not yet possible to remove it to reveal Braine's face. By pouring water into the corners of the coffin, the material slowly loosened and could be partly rolled back. As it was retracted, the face took on character and an identity.

By now they had been working for sixteen hours without rest. Beattie, aided by Damkjar, described the scene to the others as it became visible to him: 'There's a beard, curly and dark . . . got to be careful. There are the teeth, there's an ear. It looks like he's balding a bit.' Then Beattie stepped back to take in the view of a man who appeared severe and life-toughened, very much a nineteenth-century Royal Marine private. 'Look at that. After a long day's work it's really something to see,' he said quietly, as if to himself.

Braine's teeth were in very bad condition, and one of his front teeth had been broken in life, causing the exposure of the pulp. His lips, unlike Hartnell's or Torrington's, were pulled tightly over his teeth – perhaps the kerchief had prevented the lips from curling outward. His nose was slightly flattened. He would have stood 181 centimetres (nearly 6 feet) tall, and the large coffin seemed too small for him. When he had been originally placed in the coffin and the lid attached for the first time, it had pressed down onto his nose.

His eyes were deeply sunk into the eye sockets, and only one-quarter open. The eyeballs did not appear to be very well preserved, but he still had a sleepy, nearly alive appearance. A scar on his forehead indicated that he had been struck, or had cracked his head against an object, several years before his death. Finally, it was possible to remove the rest of the kerchief from the face, and they saw that his hair was nearly black, long, and partly curly, and that he was indeed bald on the front and top of his head.

After pulling the shroud away, his shirt and right arm and hand were exposed. 'Look at that hand, it's very well preserved,' Beattie said. 'Nice shirt, there's not a mark on it, it looks brand new'. No sign of his left arm could be found, and the possibility that it may have been amputated was discussed. As thawing progressed, they discovered that his left arm was frozen underneath his body. Beattie at first thought Braine had been too big to be placed in the coffin with his arms in their natural position. But they later saw that it would have been just as easy to have placed his arms over the sides of his chest and still have room for the coffin lid. His body and head, too, were not positioned carefully, and one of his undershirts had been put on backwards, leading them to conclude he was very hastily placed in the coffin.

Thawing the body was again a matter of pouring warm water over the frozen sections. In the cold of the grave the warm water would send up clouds of steam filled with the pungent smells of wet wool and cotton. Hours of this smell took its toll on some of the crew and the emotional strain of the work drained them all. Braine, being buried so deeply, was in colder ground, and the ice would not yield without a battle. They had tremendous difficulty in thawing the portions of the clothing and shroud frozen to the bottom of the coffin. Braine was trapped in his coffin by the frozen fabric, and warm water poured directly onto the material seemed to have little effect. The team struggled for eighteen more hours before they were able to free him from the ice. And even then they had to cut the clothing up the small portion of exposed back, and lift him, not only out of the coffin, but out of his clothes as well. Beattie and Amy lifted him up to the side of the grave, handing him to Savelle and Kowal who positioned him on a plastic sheet.

Immediately noticeable was the extremely emaciated appearance of this man – literally a skin-covered skeleton. Braine would have weighed less than 40 kilograms (6 stone).

Every rib could be counted, and it was possible to identify features on his hip bones. His face also reflected his condition, with the skin drawn taut over the cheeks and eye sockets. His limbs had a spidery appearance; so thin were his arms that his hands appeared very large. For Beattie, lifting this frail and lifeless man up and out of his grave, coming as it did after such tremendous effort to free him, was the most difficult aspect of his work on Beechey Island. The strained faces of the others illustrated that he was not alone in these feelings.

Exhausted though they were, Braine was immediately wrapped in a sheet and carried across to the x-ray tent. Notman and Anderson, who had been sleeping after their difficult work on Hartnell, were roused so they could begin their work.

The x-raying of Braine was carried out much as it had been with Hartnell, though the situation was quite different as Braine had not had a previous autopsy. Both worked continuously for nearly twelve hours until the x-raying was completed.

Before the others could rest they still had to remove Braine's clothing from the coffin for Schweger to analyze. With the body removed, thawing accelerated and the job was completed in an hour. During the initial thawing of the foot end of the grave Carlson thought he detected a different kind of fabric peeking out just below the shroud-wrapped feet. Not until the body had been removed, and further thawing of the shroud had taken place, was his observation confirmed. Rolled up and placed under Braine's feet were a pair of stockings. These were quite large and appeared to be of a heavy material, and one had a hole in it. The thawing and removal of the shroud and kerchief were left for the following day. Beattie, Kowal, Savelle, Amy and Damkjar wandered back to the cook tent, had a wash outside, and went in for food and drink. They were then able to have a brief rest before returning to conduct the autopsy.

When they gathered again, all suffered terrible headaches and dizzyness. Some felt they would be physically ill. They came to the conclusion that they were suffering the effects of carbon monoxide poisoning from the two stoves that burned continuously during the removal of Braine from his coffin.

Although the tent flap had been tied open and a breeze had blown through during the work, the fumes had gathered in the grave pit, creating the problem.

When Amy and Beattie entered the x-ray/autopsy tent to begin their work, Notman pointed out a series of lesions on Braine's body, on the left and right shoulders, in the groin area and along the left chest wall. These lesions involved the skin, and in some cases the tissue and muscle below. Close inspection revealed teeth marks. Notman and Amy agreed that rats must have attacked the body while it had rested aboard the *Erebus* prior to burial.

Rats were a common problem on nineteenth-century sailing ships, and caused difficulties even among arctic expeditions. Elisha Kent Kane, the United States Navy Officer, had experienced severe problems with the vermin while commanding the *Advance* in the Franklin search from 1853 to 1855:

> They are everywhere . . . under the stove, in the steward's lockers, in our cushions, about our beds. If I was asked what, after darkness and cold and scurvy, are the three besetting curses of our Arctic sojourn, I should say RATS, RATS, RATS.

> . . . it became impossible to stow anything below decks. Furs, woollens, shoes, specimens of natural history, everything we disliked to lose, however little valuable to them, was gnawed into and destroyed.

Even efforts to fumigate the ship with the 'vilest imaginable compounds of vapours – brimstone, burnt leather, and arsenic' failed to get rid of the rats.

Notman had compared the x-rays of Hartnell with those just taken of Braine and he described one interesting difference to Beattie: 'With Hartnell's skull we could not penetrate to see bony details with x-rays because of the solid block of ice inside. That's what is creating this uniform whiteness,' he said, pointing at the x-ray. 'In contrast, Braine's skull could be penetrated quite easily. I really don't have any explanation for that because they were buried under similar circumstances'.

The autopsy took seven hours, and was extremely comprehensive. Like Hartnell's, it was performed on the ground with the body resting on a sheet of white plastic. Written and recorded accounts were made during the whole period, as was a thorough photographic record. Beattie assisted Amy during the autopsy, labelling storage containers and collecting tissue samples.

Unlike either Torrington or Hartnell, Braine was partially decomposed. Green coloration of the body was an important discovery, demonstrating that some time had elapsed after William Braine's death before the burial actually took place. An explanation for this apparent delay is difficult to find although two possibilities were discussed. During the winter spent at Beechey Island, parties were sent away from the ships to survey parts of nearby Devon Island. Franklin camp sites had been discovered by searchers north of Beechey Island on the west coast of Devon Island and at Cape Riley. It is possible Braine had been on one of these parties when he died. With two graves already located at Beechey Island, his body would have been returned for burial at the tiny cemetery. Wrapped and secured to a sledge he would have frozen within a few hours, though decomposition would have already set in. When the sledge party arrived at the ships he may have been taken on board for examination by the doctors and preparation for burial. During the time spent on ship his body probably thawed, accelerating the rate of decay. Another possibility may relate to poor weather. Braine may have died when the weather did not allow his immediate burial. This seems a less reasonable explanation as the body could easily have been placed in a cool or even freezing part of the ship where the amount of observed decomposition would have been far less likely to occur.

Whatever the reason, the decomposition may at least be the explanation for Braine's body being placed quickly and without care in its coffin.

During this final autopsy, Beattie wondered what Torrington, Hartnell and Braine would have thought about what these twentieth-century investigators were doing. The three men were explorers in their own time, each one, either through conscription or by choice, involved in dangerous exploits embodying the Victorian ideals of adventure, nationalism, and self-sacrifice. Now, at least in body, they had explored through time, visiting briefly the 1980s. They could not have foretold such an odyssey.

With the autopsy and x-rays complete, a plane arrived on 20 June to pick up Amy, Notman, Anderson, Schweger and Spenceley. Those remaining on site wrapped Braine's body tightly in cotton, and lowered it to Beattie and Savelle who were standing in the grave. Gently, they laid the body in the coffin, positioning it carefully. Minutes before, Beattie had spread the shroud along the bottom of the coffin, and once the body had been placed on it, the left side of the shroud was brought over the body, followed by the right side, which was tucked underneath. The kerchief, undershirt, sweater, shirt, and stockings, each wrapped in protective mylar, were placed in the coffin and the lid lowered into position. The north side of the tent was pulled back, and the sun, low in the northern sky at 11 p.m., illuminated the headboard and inside walls of the tent. Standing beside the grave, bathed in brilliant yellow sunlight, they silently gave a moment of reflection and respect to William Braine. Beattie then jumped into the grave, and a bucket of gravel was passed down to him. He slowly emptied the bucket over the plaque, spreading the gravel in a protective layer on its surface.

Filling the grave began immediately. The huge pile of gravel, resting beside the grave, attested to the depth of the burial. Two people shovelled gravel into buckets, while the others took turns carrying the buckets to the grave and pouring them in. Soon the gravel pile began to shrink, and within three hours the grave had been filled to a point where the large rocks could be repositioned on the surface – but mental and physical exhaustion had taken hold, and this task would be completed the following day.

Several days were spent completing the restoration of the site, and after dismantling their camp, the remaining researchers left in two groups, Beattie, Nungaq and Kowal on 24 June, with Carlson, Savelle and Damkjar following on 27 June.

Other than the Franklin search expeditions of the 1850s, no others had spent so much time at the site where the crews of *Erebus* and *Terror* had experienced their first arctic winter, and the early searchers had departed with many questions still unanswered.

Beattie left Beechey Island convinced that Petty Officer Torrington, Able Seaman Hartnell, and Private Braine would provide him with some answers, for it seemed they had lived again for a few brief hours during the arctic summers of 1984 and 1986.

Chapter Thirteen

UNDERSTANDING A DISASTER

Frozen tissue, hair and bone samples from both John Hartnell and William Braine were carried back to Edmonton in a small insulated cooler, and within two days of leaving Beechey Island were stored in a deep freeze at the University of Alberta Hospital.

So much depended on this tiny box of samples. This was the evidence that would either confirm or tear apart Beattie's theory about the impact of lead on the Franklin expedition.

If trace element analysis of the samples revealed lead levels dramatically lower than had been obtained from Torrington and the Booth Point skeleton, then the source of lead exposure for those previously tested would have to be re-examined. The question would then be: why only Torrington and not the others? But if elevated levels of lead were identified during the testing of the remains of Hartnell and Braine, then a much more substantial argument could be made for the underlying impact lead would have had on the doomed expedition. Five years of research now hinged on the extraction and analysis of the information locked in the tissue samples.

Such analysis, however, takes careful planning, and in the following months while Kowal prepared to test the human samples, Beattie carefully studied the ten tin cans collected at Beechey Island.

Again there was no question that the lead contamination from the solder would have been considerable, but on closer examination the tins revealed something unexpected, something Beattie and Damkjar had overlooked while plotting and describing them on the island. The side seams of some of the tins

156

were incomplete. It appeared as if the tin smith who made them had failed properly to seal the end part of the seams. The significance of this missed step in the manufacturing process cannot be over-emphasized, as it could result in spoilage of the food contained in the tins. It is important to understand the design of the tins supplied to Franklin's expedition, both for the location of solder and the reason for the flaws.

In 1845, tinned preserved food was still a relatively recent innovation that promised immediate and major effects on exploration. The tin container itself was patented in England in 1811, and was immediately embraced by the British for use in the Royal Navy in most parts of the world. It was an invention that would allow arctic expeditions to winter successfully in the Arctic, and made an assault on the Northwest Passage seem destined for success.

The containers were constructed from a tinned wrought-iron sheet bent round a cylindrical form with the edges allowed to lap over one another. The tinsmith then placed his soldering iron on each formed seam (internal and external) and floated a bead of solder along most of its length. The seams were left unsoldered at the top and bottom ends.

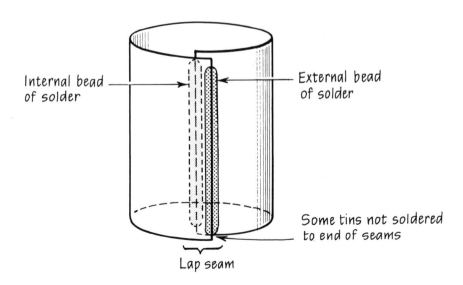

Internal bead of solder

External bead of solder

Some tins not soldered to end of seams

Lap seam

The top and bottom end pieces were bent to form a flange. When the ends were placed on the cylinder body, the flange slid over either the outside or the inside of the cylinder, depending on the tin type. The flange was the reason why the tinsmith did not solder the body lap seams all the way to the top and bottom: the end pieces could be slipped onto the cylinder body without being blocked by seam solder. However, when the ends were soldered on, the small gaps between the lap seam and the flange were not themselves always sealed with a drop of solder. The incomplete seam very likely resulted in the spoilage of some of the expedition's food supply, which supported the conclusions of some of the leading Franklin searchers.

The top end piece has a filler hole that varies in size depending on the size and type of canister. The top end piece is attached first, and is heavily soldered on the inside. The bottom end piece is then attached, and it too is soldered internally through the filler hole in the top end piece. Solder is then applied round the outside of the end seams.

Food is pushed through the filler hole, and then the tin is almost completely immersed in boiling water sometimes containing calcium chloride to increase the cooking temperature. When cooking is complete and while the food is still at temperature, the filler hole is covered by a cap which is secured with solder. The tins, now completely sealed, form a partial vacuum upon cooling. The next step is painting the outside of the tins to protect them against damage and corrosion.

The solder itself is made up of more than 90 per cent lead, wtih the balance being tin. This high lead level produces a solder which has poor 'wetting' characteristics – in other words, it does not flow very readily when in a liquid state. This means that it does not migrate easily into the spaces formed between two pieces of metal, as would solder with a higher tin content.

The contract for the tinned preserved food was given to Stephan Goldner on 1 April 1845. On 5 May, the day Franklin received his sailing instructions, the Superintendent of the Victualling Yard at Deptford reported that only one-tenth of the contract had been supplied. This was followed three days

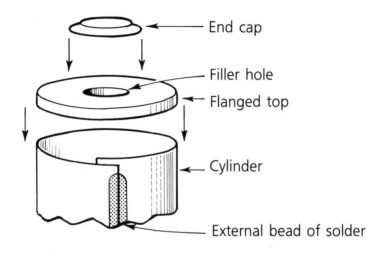

End cap

Filler hole

Flanged top

Cylinder

External bead of solder

later by a promise from Goldner that by 12 May all the meat would be delivered, and the soups by 15 May, though he did ask for and receive permission to pack the soups in tins larger than in the original specification. There is a good chance that in the rush to complete the order, quality control suffered and some food that would later spoil was included among the 8,000 tins supplied to the expedition. If a significant proportion of the food went bad, it would have added a considerable burden to the expedition. It could have meant the difference between success and failure; life and death.

As Beattie continued his research into the problem tins, Roger Amy submitted the tissues collected under sterile conditions for bacteriological assessment. The preliminary results of this research identified tuberculosis in the lung tissue of William Braine, though there had been no success in culturing the organism. But bacteria collected from the bowel of William Braine (an uncommon form of the genus *Clostridium* associated with the human bowel) was cultured. Remarkably, bacteria dating to 1846, and once part of William Braine, is still alive today.

Then, in early 1987, Walt Kowal and experts at the Alberta Workers' Health and Compensation laboratory in Edmonton began to test hair samples collected from Torrington in 1984, and Hartnell and Braine in 1986. Again the method of testing involved the combustion at high temperatures of solutions made from samples of the hair. The resulting emissions are characteristic of a particular element, such as lead, and can be identified and quantified.

The first tests were run on hair collected from the crown and nape areas of Torrington's head. They revealed levels ranging from 413 to 657 parts per million (ppm), very similar to the extremely high levels previously identified in hair samples taken from Torrington.

It wasn't until April that Kowal called Beattie with results of the first tests on Hartnell and Braine: 'Not a thing, didn't find a thing. There's nothing in the other two,' Kowal said.

Beattie was quiet for a moment and said: 'Well, now it gets more complicated'. His mind was already at work trying to figure out this new twist. But then Kowal, now laughing, quickly added: 'Wait a minute, I was pulling your leg. The levels are high, there's no denying it'.

Then came the proof Beattie had been waiting for since 1984. Hair from Hartnell yielded lead levels ranging from 138 to 313 ppm, while hair from Braine was very similar at 145 to 280 ppm. Although not as high as the lead levels measured in Torrington, they exceeded a contemporary hair standard by well over twenty times. Subsequent testing eliminated the possibility of external twentieth-century contamination, and further tests on bone and tissue from Torrington, Hartnell and Braine underscored the accuracy of the hair results.

The fact that the information on lead exposure came from hair meant that the contamination occurred during Franklin's voyage, and not from industrial pollution in the British environment of the day. Possible sources of lead exposure on the expedition were numerous, including tea wrapped in lead foil, pewterware, and lead-glazed pottery vessels. But it was the reliance of Franklin's expedition on tinned food that was the root cause. It has been calculated that each sailor would have been allotted about half a pound (¼ kg) of tinned food every second day, resulting in regular and considerable ingestion of lead.

There can be no exact explanation of the differences in the level of lead between Torrington on the one hand, and Hartnell and Braine on the other. It is quite likely related to differences in the food consumed by the three men, and their jobs aboard ship. For example, Torrington, as leading stoker, may have picked up added contamination from lead in coal dust.

What is very clear from the findings, now based on four (including the Booth Point skeleton) separate individuals and using the facilities of a series of different labs, is that lead played an important role in the declining health of the entire crews of the *Erebus* and *Terror*, not only in the loss of physical energy but increasingly in the mind's despair. Loss of appetite, fatigue, weakness and colic are some of the physical symptoms of lead poisoning; it can also cause disturbances of the central and peripheral nervous systems, producing neurotic and erratic behaviour and paralysis of the limbs. It is the effects on the mind that may have been of greatest importance in isolating the impact of lead on the expedition. Under the continuing and prolonged stressful conditions of long periods in the Arctic, even very subtle effects of low lead exposure could have had significant impact on the decision-making processes of the men, particularly the officers. Only clear minds in control of situations can hope to make correct decisions.

There is no single reason why the expedition failed; it was a deadly combination of factors. That is why there is no one answer to the question of what caused the Franklin expedition disaster. Perhaps the best that can be done today is to isolate the reasonable possibilities and fit them into the broad circumstances that are identified from scattered remains found at archaeological sites. That is what Beattie was able to do.

In some cases, such as the three sailors from Beechey Island, the effects of lead poisoning were catastrophic. Amy's autopsy results showed that, like Torrington, both Hartnell and Braine suffered from tuberculosis and died from pneumonia. In addition, radiological evidence obtained by Derek Notman identified a collapsed eleventh thoracic vertebra in William Braine, a condition caused by Pott's disease which in turn is usually caused by tubercular infection. But it was the insidious and poorly understood poison, lead, entering their bodies at high levels over the course of the first months of the expedition that weakened these three young men to the point that they were easily killed off by supervening diseases.

Other crewmen would have been as severely affected by the poisoning, which probably explains at least some of the other twenty-one deaths experienced by the expedition in the early period before the ships were deserted on 22 April 1848.

As for the high ratio of officer deaths prior to the death march, nine of the twenty-one, Beattie found possible explanations consistent with the lead findings. If the officers, a rigidly separated and very aloof class, even during long and confined expeditions, were using their pewter tableware and eating a preferential food source (that is, proportionately more tinned food), they may have ingested much higher levels of lead than the other seamen. It is at least possible that Sir John Franklin himself died directly or indirectly from the effects of lead poisoning.

As for those men who died during the tragic death march in the spring and summer of 1848, some may have exhibited classic symptoms of the poisoning, such as anorexia, weakness and fatigue, and paranoia, which would have compounded the effects of starvation and scurvy. Other crewmen may not have shown any obvious effects of the poison, perhaps because of differing diets and physical response to the lead.

It is sadly ironic that Franklin's mighty expedition, certainly one of the greatest seafaring expeditions ever launched, carrying all the tools that early industry and innovation could offer, should have been mortally wounded by one of them. Yet Beattie believes he has the scientific evidence to say that is so.

When Sir John Franklin sailed from the Thames in May 1845, an entire nation believed that the honour of conquering the Northwest Passage was within his grasp. None could have known that inside the tins stored in the ship's hold there ticked a timebomb that helped not only to deny Franklin his triumph, but to steal away 129 brave lives. And while good hopes decayed in a relatively short time for the expedition crews, the physicians aboard the *Erebus* and *Terror* would have been helpless to intervene. The health risks imposed by the use of lead-tin solder were simply not appreciated at that time. It was not until 1890 that government legislation in Britain finally banned soldering on the insides of food tins.

There is often a terrible price to pay in human exploration reliant upon new technology. That fact was vividly demonstrated again only recently by the failure of the space shuttle *Challenger*.

Indeed our explorers of space share a bond with past explorers of the unknown frozen shores of the earth. In many ways there is no difference between the Franklin and space shuttle disasters. Time, technology, social conditions, and politics have changed, but the spirit and motivation underlying both endeavours remain. Both used the most advanced technology of their time and both paid the ultimate price. An article published in an 1855 edition of *Blackwood's Edinburgh Magazine* lamented those dangers:

> We confess we have not heart enough, in the general enterprise of knowledge, to view such a sacrifice as that of Franklin and his crew without a chill of horror: there is something frightful, inexorable, inhuman, in prosecuting researches, which are mere researches, after such a costly fashion . . . and when we hear of the martyrs of science, whether they perish among the arctic snow or the sands of the desert, we begin to think of science herself as a placid Juggernaut . . . with benevolent pretensions, winning, by some weird magic, and throwing away with all the calmness of an abstract and impersonal principle, those generous lives.

These thoughts, published even before M'Clintock made his grisly discoveries, could have been written in response to Beattie's. But such conclusions dwell only on the failure of science and technology and deny the achievements. For after Franklin, others followed. They too used the latest technology available to them, and they succeeded not only in tracing a Northwest Passage, but in conquering the last and most forbidding land on earth.

APPENDIX ONE

List of the officers and crew of HMS *Erebus* and *Terror* taken from their Muster Books, 1845.
Source: Admiralty Records, Public Record Office.

HMS *Erebus*

CAPTAIN Sir John Franklin

COMMANDER James Fitzjames

LIEUTENANTS Graham Gore, H. T. D. Le Vesconte, James W. Fair-holme

MATES Robert O. Sargent, Charles F. Des Voeux, Edward Couch

SECOND MASTER Henry F. Collins

SURGEON Stephen S. Stanley

ACTING ASSISTANT-SURGEON Harry D. S. Goodsir

PAYMASTER AND PURSER Charles H. Osmer

ACTING MASTER James Reid

WARRANT OFFICERS John Gregory (engineer), Thomas Terry (boatswain), John Weekes (carpenter)

PETTY OFFICERS Philip Reddington (captain of the forecastle), Thomas Watson (carpenter's mate), John Murray (sailmaker), James W. Brown (caulker), William Smith (blacksmith), Samuel

Brown (boatswain's mate), Richard Wall (cook), James Rigden (captain's coxswain), John Sullivan (captain of the maintop), Robert Sinclair (captain of the foretop), Joseph Andrews (captain of the hold), Edmund Hoar (captain's steward), Richard Aylmore (gunroom steward), Daniel Arthur (quartermaster), John Downing (quartermaster), William Bell (quartermaster), Francis Dunn (caulker's mate), William Fowler (paymaster and purser's steward), John Bridgens (subordinate officers' steward), James Hart (leading stoker), John Cowie (stoker), Thomas Plater (stoker)

ABLE SEAMEN Henry Lloyd, John Stickland, Thomas Hartnell, **John Hartnell**, George Thompson, William Orren, Charles Coombs, William Closson, William Mark, Thomas Work, Charles Best, George Williams, John Morfin, Thomas Tadman, Abraham Seely, Thomas McConvey, Robert Ferrier, Josephus Geater, Robert Johns, Francis Pocock

ROYAL MARINES David Bryant (sergeant), Alexander Paterson (corporal), Joseph Healey (private), **William Braine** (private), William Reed (private), Robert Hopcraft (private), William Pilkington (private)

BOYS George Chambers, David Young

HMS *Terror*

CAPTAIN Francis Rawdon Moira Crozier

LIEUTENANTS Edward Little, John Irving, George H. Hodgson

MATES Robert Thomas, Frederick John Hornby

SECOND MASTER Gillies A. Macbean

SURGEON John S. Peddie

ASSISTANT SURGEON Alexander MacDonald

CLERK-IN-CHARGE E. J. H. Helpman

ACTING MASTER Thomas Blanky

WARRANT OFFICERS Thomas Honey (carpenter), John Lane (boatswain), James Thompson (engineer)

PETTY OFFICERS Reuben Male (captain of the forecastle), Thomas Johnson (boatswain's mate), **John Torrington** (leading stoker), Alexander Wilson (carpenter's mate), David MacDonald (quartermaster), William Rhodes (quartermaster), John Kenley (quartermaster), Thomas Darlington (caulker), John Diggle (cook), Thomas Farr (captain of the maintop), Henry Peglar (captain of the foretop), John Wilson (captain's coxswain), Samuel Honey (blacksmith), William Goddard (captain of the hold), Thomas Jopson (captain's steward), Thomas Armitage (gunroom steward), Cornelius Hickey (caulker's mate), Edward Genge (paymaster's steward), William Gibson (subordinate officers' steward), Luke Smith (stoker), William Johnson (stoker)

ABLE SEAMEN George Cann, William Shanks, David Sims, William Sinclair, William Jerry, Henry Sait, Alexander Berry, John Bailey, Samuel Crispe, John Bates, William Wentzall, William Strong, John Handford, Charles Johnson, David Leys, George Kinnaird, Magnus Manson, James Walker, Edwin Laurence

ROYAL MARINES Solomon Tozer (sergeant), William Hedges (corporal), Henry Wilks (private), John Hammond (private), James Daly (private), William Heather (private)

BOYS Robert Golding, Thomas Evans

Four crewmen who returned to Britain on the *Barretto Junior* and the *Rattler* before the *Erebus* and *Terror* entered the Arctic: Thomas Burt (armourer), John Brown (able seaman), James Elliot (sailmaker), William Aitken (Royal Marine private)

APPENDIX TWO

Major expeditions involved in the search for HMS *Erebus* and HMS *Terror*:

1846-47 Dr John Rae (overland)
1847-49 Sir John Richardson and Dr John Rae (overland)
1848-49 Capt.Sir James Clark Ross, Capt.E.J.Bird, (HMS *Enterprise* & HMS *Investigator*)
1848-50 Capt. Henry Kellett (HMS *Herald*)
1848-52 Capt. Thomas Moore (HMS *Plover*)
1849-50 Lieut. James Saunders (HMS *North Star*)
1850-51 U.S. Navy Lieut. Edwin J. De Haven, U.S. Navy Lieut. S.P. Griffin (*Advance* & *Rescue*)
1850-51 Capt. Horatio Austin, Capt. Erasmus Ommanney, Lieut. Sherard Osborn, Lieut. Bertie Cator (HMS *Resolute*, HMS *Assistance*, HMS *Intrepid*, HMS *Pioneer*)*
1850-51 Capt. William Penny, Alexander Stewart (*Lady Franklin* and *Sophia*)*
1850-51 Rear Admiral Sir John Ross (*Felix*)
1850 Captain C.C. Forsyth (*Prince Albert*)
1850-55 Capt. Richard Collinson (HMS *Enterprise*)
1850-54 Commander Robert McClure (HMS *Investigator*)
1851 Dr John Rae (overland)
1851-52 Capt. William Kennedy (*Prince Albert*)
1852 Commander Edward Augustus Inglefield (*Isabel*)
1852-54 Capt. Sir Edward Belcher, Sherard Osborn, Capt. Henry Kellett, Commander Francis Leopold M'Clin-

tock (HMS *Assistance. * HMS *Pioneer,* HMS *Resolute,* HMS *Intrepid*)

1852-54 William John Samuel Pullen (HMS *North Star*)

1853 Capt. Edward Augustus Inglefield, William Fawckner (HMS *Phoenix* & HMS *Breadalbane*)

1853-54 Dr John Rae (overland)★

1853-55 U.S. Navy Dr. Elisha Kent Kane (*Advance*)

1855 Chief Factor John Anderson (overland)

1857-59 Capt. Francis Leopold M'Clintock, Lieut. William Robert Hobson (*Fox*)★

1869 Charles Francis Hall (overland)★

1878-80 U.S. Lieut. Frederick Schwatka (overland)★

★ Made significant discoveries of Franklin expedition relics

BIBLIOGRAPHY

There are, literally, millions of details relating to the preparation for, and loss of the 1845-8 Franklin expedition and the subsequent searches. The following bibliography is not definitive, but it does include sources which will allow the reader to explore the complexities of historical and scientific research into the disaster. Each of the entries has been used by the authors as information and/or illustration sources.

Amundsen, R. 1908 *The North West Passage*. Constable, London.

Amy, R., Bahatnagar, R., Damkjar E., and Beattie, O., 1986 The last Franklin expedition: report of a postmortem examination of a crew member. *Canadian Medical Association Journal* 135:115-117.

Anderson, J.E., and Merbs, C.F., 1962 A contribution to the human osteology of the Canadian Arctic. Occasional Paper 4, Art and Archaeology Division, Royal Ontario Museum, University of Toronto.

Back, George 1838 *Narrative of an Expedition in H.M.S. Terror Undertaken with a View to Geographical Discovery on the Arctic Shores in the Years 1836-7*. John Murray, London.

Beattie, O.B., and Savelle, J.M. 1983 Discovery of human remains from Sir John Franklin's last expedition. *Historical Archaeology* 17:100-105.

Beattie, O.B., 1983 A report on newly discovered human skeletal remains from the last Sir John Franklin expedition. *The Muskox* 33:68-77.

Beattie, O.B., Damkjar, E., Kowal, W., Amy, R., 1985 Anatomy of an arctic autopsy. *Medical Post* 20(23):1-2.

Belcher, E. 1855 *The Last of the Arctic Voyages.* Lovell Reeve, London.

Bernier, Joseph E. 1909 Report on the Dominion Government Expedition to Arctic Islands and Hudson Strait, on Board the D.G.S. 'Arctic'. Government Printing Bureau, Ottawa.

Busch, Jane 1981 An introduction to the tin can. *Historical Archaeology* 15:95-104.

Cooke, Alan, and Holland, Clive 1978 *The Exploration of Northern Canada.* Arctic History Press, Toronto.

Cooper, P.F. 1955 A trip to King William Island in 1954. *The Arctic Circular* VIII, no. 1.

Cyriax, Richard J. 1939 *Sir John Franklin's Last Arctic Expedition.* Methuen, London.

Cyriax, Richard J. 1951 Recently discovered traces of the Franklin expedition. *Geographical Journal*, June, pp. 211-14.

Cyriax, Richard J. 1952 The position of Victory Point, King William Island. *Polar Record* 6:496-507.

Cyriax, Richard J. 1958 The two Franklin Expedition records found on King William Island. *The Mariner's Mirror* 44:178-189.

Cyriax, Richard J. 1962 Adam Beck and the Franklin search. *The Mariner's Mirror* 48:35-51.

Cyriax, R.J., and Jones, A.G.E., 1954 The papers in the possession of Harry Peglar, Captain of the Foretop, H.M.S. Terror, 1845. *The Mariner's Mirror* 40:186-195.

Francis, Daniel 1986 *The Discovery of the North.* Hurtig, Edmonton.

Franklin, John 1823 *Narrative of a Journey to the Shores of the Polar Sea, in the years 1819, 20, 21, and 22. With an Appendix on Various Subjects Relating to Science and Natural History.* John Murray, London.

Franklin, John 1828 *Narrative of a Second Expedition to the Shores of the Polar Sea, in the Years 1825, 1826, and 1827, by Sir John Franklin; including an account of the Progress of a Detachment to the Eastward by John Richardson.* John Murray, London.

Gibson, William 1932 Some further traces of the Franklin retreat. *Geographical Journal* 79:402-08.

BIBLIOGRAPHY

Gibson, William 1933 The Dease and Simpson cairn. *The Beaver* 264:44-45.

Gibson, William 1937 Sir John Franklin's last voyage. *The Beaver* 268:44-75.

Gilder, W.H. 1881 *Schwatka's Search*. Scribner's Sons, New York.

Glob, P.V. 1969 *The Bog People*. Faber and Faber, London.

Gzowski, P. 1981 *The Sacrament*. McClelland and Stewart, Toronto.

Holland, Clive 1980 Franklin expedition and search. In: The Discoverers; an Encyclopedia of Explorers and Exploration, H. Delpar, editor. McGraw-Hill, New York.

Huntford, Roland 1979 *The Last Place on Earth*. Pan Books, London.

Inglefield, E.A. 1852 Unpublished letter to Sir Francis Beaufort, dated 14 September 1852.

Inglefield, E.A. 1853 *A Summer Search for Sir John Franklin with a Peep into a Polar Basin*. Thomas Harrison and Son, London.

International Tin Research and Development Council 1939 *Historic Tinned Foods*. International Tin Research and Development Council Publication Number 85 (Second Edition), Greenford, Middlesex.

Johnson, R.E., Johnson, M.H., Jeanes, H.S., and Deaver, S.M. 1984 *Schwatka: The Life of Frederick Schwatka (1849-1892), M.D., Arctic Explorer, Cavalry Officer*. Horn of the Moon, Montpelier.

Kane, Elisha Kent 1853 *The U.S. Grinnell Expedition in Search of Sir John Franklin*. Harper and Brothers, New York.

Kane, Elisha Kent 1856 *Arctic Explorations: The Second Grinnell Expedition in Search of Sir John Franklin, 1853, '54, '55*. Childs and Peterson, Philadelphia.

Kane, Elisha Kent 1898 *Arctic Explorations in Search of Sir John Franklin*. T. Nelson and Sons, London.

Lind, James 1753 *A Treatise on Scurvy*. Facsimile edition (1953), C.P. Stewart and D. Guthrie, ed. Edinburgh University Press

Loomis, C.C. 1971 *Weird & Tragic Shores*. Macmillan, London.

MacInnis, Joe 1985 *The Land That Devours Ships*. CBC Enterprises, Toronto.

M'Clintock, F.L. 1908 *The Voyage of the 'Fox' In Arctic Seas*.

John Murray, London.

M'Dougall, George Frederick 1857 *The Eventful Voyage of H.M. Discovery Ship 'Resolute' to the Arctic Regions, in Search of Sir John Franklin and the Missing Crew of H.M. Discovery ships 'Erebus' and 'Terror', 1852, 1853, 1854.* Longman, Brown, Green, Longmans and Roberts, London.

Markham, A.H. 1891 *Life of Sir John Franklin and the North-West Passage.* G. Philip, London.

Martin, Constance 1983 *James Hamilton: Arctic Watercolours.* Glenbow Museum, Calgary.

Murchison, R. 1853 Commander E.A. Inglefield – Royal Awards. *Journal of the Royal Geographical Society* 23: pp.ix–ixi.

Nanton, Paul 1970 *Arctic Breakthrough.* Clarke, Irwin & Co., Toronto.

Neatby, L.H. 1958 *In Quest of the Northwest Passage.* Longmans, Green and Company, Toronto.

Neatby, L.H. 1970 *Search for Franklin.* Hurtig, Edmonton.

Newman, Peter C. 1985 *Company of Adventurers.* Penguin Books, Markham.

Notman, D., Anderson, L., Beattie, O., and Amy, R., n.d. Arctic paleoradiology: portable x-ray examination of two frozen sailors from the Franklin expedition (1845-48). *American Journal of Roentgenology*: accepted in April, 1987.

Nourse, J.E. (editor) 1879 *Narrative of the Second Arctic Expedition of C.F. Hall.* United States Naval Observatory, Washington.

Osborn, Sherard 1865 *Stray Leaves from an Arctic Journal; or, Eighteen Months in the Polar Regions, in Search of Sir John Franklin's Expedition, in the Years 1850-51.* Longman, Brown, Green, and Longmans, London.

Osborn, Sherard (editor) 1857 *The Discovery of the North-West Passage by HMS 'Investigator', Capt. R. M'Clure. 1850, 1851, 1852, 1853, 1854, Second Edition.* Longman, Brown, Green, Longmans and Roberts, London.

Owen, Roderic 1978 *The Fate of Franklin.* Hutchinson, London.

Parry, William Edward 1821 *Journal of a Voyage for the Discovery of a North-West Passage from the Atlantic to the Pacific; Performed in the Years 1819-20, in His Majesty's Ships 'Hecla' and 'Griper'.* John Murray, London.

Rae, John 1855 Arctic exploration, with information respecting Sir John Franklin's missing party. *Journal of the Royal Geographical Society* 25:246-56.

Rasmussen, K. 1927 *Across Arctic America: Narrative of the Fifth Thule Expedition.* G.P. Putnam's Sons, New York.

Read, P.P. 1974 *Alive: the Story of the Andes Survivors.* Avon Books, New York.

Roland, Charles G. 1984 Saturnism at Hudson's Bay: The York Factory Complaint of 1833-1836. *Canadian Bulletin of Medical History* 1:59-78.

Ross, John 1835 *Narrative of a Second Voyage in Search of Northwest Passage, and of a Residence in the Arctic Regions.* A.W. Webster, London.

Shelley, Mary 1980 *Frankenstein.* Oxford, Toronto.

Simpson, Thomas 1843 *Narrative of the Discoveries on the North Coast of America: Effected by the Officers of the Hudson's Bay Company During the Years 1836-39.* Richard Bentley, London.

Stackpole, E.A. (editor) 1965 *The Long Arctic Search: The Narrative of Lieutenant Frederick Schwatka, U.S.A., 1878-1880.* Marine Historical Association, Mystic.

Stefansson, V. 1939 *Unsolved Mysteries of the Arctic.* New York.

Sutherland, Patricia D. (editor) 1985 *The Franklin Era in Canadian Arctic History, 1845-1859.* Mercury Series Archaeological Survey of Canada Paper No. 131, National Museums of Canada, Ottawa.

Sutherland, Peter 1852 *Journal of a Voyage in Baffin's Bay and Barrow Straits, in the Years 1850-1851, performed by H.M. Ships 'Lady Franklin' and 'Sophia', under the Command of Mr William Penny, in Search of the Missing Crews of H.M. Ships 'Erebus' and 'Terror'.* Longman, Brown, Green, and Longmans, London.

Wallis, Helen 1984 England's Search for the Northern Passages in the Sixteenth and Early Seventeenth Centuries. *Arctic* Vol. 37, No. 4.

Watt, J., Freeman, E.J., and Bynum, W.F., 1981 *Starving Sailors: the Influence of Nutrition Upon Naval and Maritime History.* National Maritime Museum, Bristol.

Wonders, W.C. 1968 Search for Franklin. *Canadian Geographical Journal* 76:116-27.

Woodward, F.J. 1951 *Portrait of Jane: A Life of Lady Franklin.* Hodder and Stoughton, London.

Wright, Noel 1959 *Quest for Franklin.* London.

Young, Allen 1879 *The Two Voyages of the Pandora in 1875 and 1876.* Edward Stanford, London.

Newspapers and magazines used include:

Blackwood's Edinburgh Magazine, November 1855

Edmonton Journal, 9 September 1930

Edmonton Sun, 24 September 1984, 26 September 1984, 21 October 1984

Illustrated London News, 24 May 1845, 12 October 1850, 18 February 1854, 28 October 1854, 15 October 1859, 1 January 1881

The Times, 26 April 1845, 12 May 1845, 23 December 1851, 3 January 1852

Toronto Globe 4 April 1850, 30 April 1850, 23 October 1854, 25 October 1854, 11 October 1859

Other material was derived from various Parliamentary Papers of Great Britain (post-1847), the Arctic Blue Books, the Muster Books of the *Erebus* and *Terror*, Public Record Office (UK), and the collection of the Hydrographic Department, Ministry of Defence (UK) for the letter from Inglefield to Beaufort, 14 September 1852.

INDEX

175

INDEX

INDEX

29, 126-7
character 15, 17, 127
death 38, 40, 48, 68, 162
early career 9-11, 49
knighthood 10
Franklin, Sir John, and the
    search for the Northwest
    Passage 5, 15, 41, 43
disappearance 19-21, 28
first traces found 21, 22
last contact 18
memorials 34, *43*, 46-7, 49,
    100
sole written record found *35*,
    36-8, *37*
see also artefacts and debris;
    Erebus, HMS and *Terror*,
    HMS; expeditions in
    search of Franklin
Franklin Point 68
Franklin Strait 41
Frobisher, Martin 6
fuel 12, 64, 65, 76
fur traders 15-16, 27

Gibson, William 57
Gilbert, W.E. 50
Gjoa 49, 119
Gjoa Haven 53, 64
Gladman Point: DEW 57-8
Goldner, Stephen 25, 113,
    158-9
Goodsir, Harry D.S. 140-2,
    141, 143-4
Gore, Graham 36, *37*, 38, 73
Gore Point 71-3
gravel 73-4, 93, 94, 97
    over graves 95, 154
    in tin cans 25, 112-3
graves
    Beechey Island: three 22-6,
        *24; for Beattie's
        investigations see under*
        Braine, William; Hartnell,
        John; Torrington, John
    Cape Seafort 53, 57
    dummy memorial graves 96,
        99
    Irving and Le Vesconte
        removed from Arctic for
        burial 46
    Schwatka's discoveries 46-7,
        47
    of searchers 99
Great Fish River (renamed Back
    River) 28, 30, 34, 38, 39,
    61
Greenhithe, London 5, 16
Greenwich Hospital: memorial
    46-7
Griffiths, Edward 17
Grinnell, Henry 21, 27
guns
    Beattie's 52, 64, 65, 142-3

Franklin's 18, 25, 39, 48

Hair analysis 85, 123, 156, 159-
    60
Hall, Charles Francis 43-5, *44*,
    54, 60, 86
hare 75
Harlestone, Margaret (Mrs.
    Parker) 52-4
Hartnell family: letters 128-9
Hartnell, John: grave 22-6, *24*
    Beattie's investigations
        (1984) 85-7, 91-2, 111-2,
        113-6, 118-9; earlier
        opening 112, 113-8, 134-5
    Beattie's investigations
        (1986, exhumation,
        autopsy and reburial) 131-
        45, 153-4; announcement
        locates descendants 128-9;
        cap 116, 135, 136; cause of
        death 143, 144, 161;
        clothing 114, 135, 136,
        139-40, 145; earlier
        autopsy (at death) 140-2;
        face 115-6; laboratory
        analysis 156, 159-61;
        refreezing 134; shroud
        116, 135, 137, 144
Hartnell, Thomas (brother of
    John) 114-5, 136, 145
headboards of graves 23-4, 93,
    126, 127
Hearne, Samuel 8
Hiqiniq, Kovic 53, 56-7, 57-8
Hobson, William Robert 34-41,
    35, 69, 73
Honey, Thomas 125-6
Hudson Bay exploration 6-7
    see also Northwest Passage
Hudson's Bay Company 7-8
    Franklin 15-16, 61; search 21,
    28, 29
human remains, skeletons
    King William Island 45, 73;
    Booth Point skeleton 3-4,
        54-6, 113, 123, 156, 161;
    Inuit graves 57, 58;
    lifeboat *31*, 38-9, 46, 79-
        82; Peglar 35
    physical anthropology 50,
        51, 55-6
    20th century work; skeleton
        moved to Museum in
        Ottawa 49-50
    see also cannibalism;
        laboratory analysis;
        preservation; soft tissue
        (human)

Ice: in graves 96, 102, 103, 104,
    133
    inside coffins 104-5, 133-4,
        148, 150; bodies refrozen

110, 131, 131-2, 134
Ice: sea ice 5, 42-3, 72
    Erebus and *Terror*: reinforced
        9, 12; trapped 28-9, 38, 41,
        42-3
    other ships trapped 34, 101
illness, injury and death, in
    expeditions 6-7, 8, 25, 58,
    65, 99
illness, injury and death . . .
    Franklin 15, 25, 26, 117
    causes investigated by
        Beattie 52, 58, 70-1;
    Beechey Island graves 9,
        156, 160-2; health risk at
        exhumation 86, 101-2; *see
        also* Braine, William;
        Hartnell, John;
        Torrington, John
    last to die 62
    officer cf. seamen 70-1, 125,
        162
    see also laboratory analysis;
        lead and lead poisoning
Illustrated London News 15, 21,
    28, 40-1, 43, 48
Inglefield, Edward Augustus
    27, 116-8, 134-5
Inuit 8, 28, 44-5, 48-9, 50, 53,
    75
    in Beattie's investigations 53-
        4, 63
    human remains 57, 58, 86
    old sites 54, 69-70
    reports on Franklin
        expedition 29-30, 34, 44-
        5, 47-8, 58-9; to Queen
        Victoria 28
Investigator, HMS (McClure)
    20, 27, 99
Irving, John 46-7, *47*, 69
    note under cairn 36-8, *37*
Isabel 27, 116-8

Jackson, A.Y. 100
Jones Sound 20, 27

Kane, Elisha Kent 23-4, *24*, 27,
    152
Kellet, Henry 19
Kennedy, William 27, 99
King William Island 66
    Beattie 50, 52-62, 63-82,
    Franklin 30, 41-3; searches:
        (Hall) 43-5, 50,
        (M'Clintock and Hobson)
        34-41, *35*, 50, (Rae) 21,
        29, (Schwatka) 43-8, 50
King William's Land 42
Knight, James 7-8
Kowal, Walt 159-60
    (1982) 63, 65, 71-2, 76-9, 82
    (1984) 91-2; Hartnell 111,
        113-5, 119; Torrington 96,

177

INDEX

INDEX

179

A NOTE ON THE AUTHORS

Owen Beattie PhD was born in Victoria, British Columbia, and is Associate Professor of Anthropology at the University of Alberta, Canada. As part of a long-term investigation into the effects of diet and environment on the health of nineteenth-century European explorers, he is director and principal investigator of the Franklin project. He is married and lives in Alberta with his wife and three children.

John Grigsby Geiger was born in Ithaca, New York in 1960 and was educated at the University of Alberta, where he graduated in History. He is currently a writer for the Edmonton Journal and is based in Alberta. As a journalist, Geiger was awarded the Edward Dunlop Award of Excellence in 1984 for his coverage of the scientific investigations into the fate of the Franklin expedition.